UN-HINGED

www.mascotbooks.com

Un-Hinged: What I Learned from Saying, "It's You, It's Not Me" in the NYC Dating Scene

For more information, please contact:
Mascot Books
620 Herndon Parkway, Suite 320
Herndon, VA 20170
info@mascotbooks.com

I have tried to recreate events, locales, and conversations from my memories of them. In order to maintain their anonymity in some instances I have changed the names of individuals and places. I may have changed some identifying characteristics and details such as physical properties, occupations, and places of residence.

Library of Congress Control Number: 2021915019

CPSIA Code: PRV1021A
ISBN-13: 978-1-63755-023-6

Printed in the United States

*To all the men who swiped right on my Hinge profile,
and to all the single women who haven't found their match,
this one's for you.*

UN-HINGED
WHAT I LEARNED FROM SAYING,
"IT'S YOU, IT'S NOT ME"
IN THE NYC DATING SCENE

MARIANN YIP

Artwork by Deanna First

CONTENTS

PREFACE

I DON'T EVEN KNOW where to begin when it comes to explaining my dating history and experience in NYC. It's truly been a roller coaster ride, and I never thought I would be here today, recounting all the men I've met over the two years on the only dating app I took a chance on, *Hinge*.

Hinge is known as the *"app that's designed to be deleted."* I will say from my own experience, I do think it's one of the better dating apps out there. I've never downloaded Tinder, since that has a bad reputation—it's known for hookups—and I've dabbled in Bumble and Coffee Meets Bagel, but they just didn't do it for me.

What I like about Hinge is its interface and its focus on prompts because if you're looking for a relationship with some substance, you're going to want to bypass just the looks and get to know someone for who they are at their core. I was intrigued by all the profiles I came across. The profiles that stood out to me the most were ones that made their personalities shine through. While looks matter, I was more interested in seeing whether we would be compatible, especially if these were prospects whom I would consider meeting in person. And I'm a sucker for witty banter or clever conversation starters. So, even if their profiles didn't necessarily catch my attention at first glance, I would give men with amusing opening lines a chance because I knew going into this whole online dating culture that I would keep an open mind and not be too quick to swipe left.

Let's backtrack a little, so you can understand why I, a twenty-nine-year-old sassy native New Yorker who's always preaching about independence and not needing a man, found myself creating a profile on a dating app, something that I never thought I would have to do *to find love.*

Several years before, I was in a long-term relationship with the love of my life—or so I thought at the time. I met him during the summer of 2013 when I was twenty-one years old at The DL, a lounge that you might be familiar with if you live in New York. It was actually the first year that the DL opened, and I will spare you all the details of that evening. But I will be honest that I didn't want to go out at all that night, and I didn't expect to meet someone either.

I was also in the state of mind of being young, wild, and free, and I had no intentions of having a boyfriend. Out of all my friends, I was more of the anti-relationship type of gal because I loved my freedom so much. And let's be real, at age twenty-one, who is actually looking for a relationship? I didn't think anything would come out of this summer fling because I was entering my senior year of college and was somewhat done with my party phase. Besides, I was never a fan of long-distance relationships or feeling tied down to someone who wasn't even remotely close to me. I attended Syracuse University, and he lived in Long Island, so you can imagine how difficult that was to maintain a healthy relationship considering my love language is quality time.

But lo and behold, we entered into a serious relationship, which lasted a little over three years. There's a lot that I can unpack from that relationship, but this book isn't about the breakup. Our relationship ended because we grew apart and didn't grow together. And quite frankly, I'm not bitter about it at all. The breakup taught me a lot about love, about what I don't want in a relationship, about what I do want in a relationship and made me realize that being alone is actually better than being unhappy with somebody. Most importantly, the breakup taught me how to be a better communicator and partner for someone in the future.

I truly believe that people enter your life for a reason, and then the relationship ends when they no longer serve you. This concept can be applied to everything in life, from friendships and acquaintances, to jobs and projects, and even to the places you call home. Once it stops serving you, and once you stop feeling fulfilled, that's when you know, *you have to move on.*

After the breakup, I embarked on my first solo trip to Sweden and dedicated one year to myself; 2017 was my year to be selfish. I like to think of that year as a transformational year where I dated myself. I spent a lot of time getting to know myself by being comfortable in my own company, thoughts, and feelings. Through my solitude, I felt complete as an individual because I ultimately found myself. It was after my soul-searching and self-work that I felt ready to put myself out there again, which brings us to my decision to give online dating a chance. Not only since online dating is basically the norm for our society today in terms of meeting someone, but I saw the success in several of my friends' relationships, and that gave me hope. My best friend met her husband on Tinder (shocker, I know!), another one met her husband through JSwipe, and a few others met their significant others on Hinge. I thought to myself, *If it works for them, then it can work for me too!*

I was excited about this dating process, and I wanted to have fun with it. Looking back, especially during the first few months when I was on the app, I had no idea what I was getting myself into. I didn't know what I was doing, and it clearly showed in my actions and how I handled some dates and situations. But I have no regrets because they all taught me valuable lessons and the experiences all proved to be useful data for this book.

To date, I have over 243 matches on Hinge (not counting the ones who deleted their profiles, found their person, or unmatched with me). I say this not to brag, but to give you an idea of how many conversations and men I have come across on the app. Of course, I didn't go on 243 dates, but if I'm going to be honest,

I actually can't even remember how many dates I've been on because, yes, it's been that many!

I've heard horror stories from people when it comes to online dating and mostly more from men than women, but I feel like my experience has been more on the positive side. I've never actually had a bad first date. I've had one person who was somewhat of a "catfish," but even then, I still stuck it out because I'm just too nice of a person to cut a date short even if I'm not feeling it. I try to still make the most of any dates because if you're already there, why not? I'd like to also think that you can learn something new from every person you come across, so I try to be present despite knowing a guy I'm on a date with isn't my person.

For the most part, I had great dates because I try to show the best version of myself and I actually enjoy the process of getting to know someone new. I've also been told multiple times that I'm a positive ball of energy and that my energy is contagious, so it wasn't common to not have a good time with me. Yes, I know that sounds a bit egotistic, but ladies, it's important and totally fine to acknowledge what you bring to the table!

I've also come to realize that the first three dates are technically bullshit. Most first dates are at a bar, and once you have a few drinks in your system, you're a little more loose and comfortable. This setting makes the conversation more natural and effortless. Let's not forget that the dark lighting and intimate vibe make you feel closer to the other person, and the date usually ends on a positive note. The second date is like the first date, except you're confirming whether that interest and connection is still there. The third date is when you decide if you want to continue to see this person or not. If they normally make it past the third date, then they qualify to be a running candidate in your own version of the *Bachelorette*. At least, that's how it all played out in my mind.

It's totally normal to casually date and juggle men because why put all your eggs in one basket, am I right? But in my experience, I found that there were normally two men, three at most, who I would see at a time (all of whom I had more than two dates at this point) because otherwise, it would be too much to maintain. Dating is like a job, and you have to actually put some energy and work into it. And ugh, who has time for that? Dating more than one man also proved a bit difficult when it came to remembering all the details, like how many siblings they have, where their family is from, what their favorite movie is, etc.

The common timeline for my dating history would go like this: I would either have two to three guys that are competing for the final rose, a guy would win my first impression rose, thus I would see him exclusively until the relationship fizzled, or I would go on this streak of one to two off dates with these lame-ass men, and nothing would really stick.

If you can relate and have been on the same boat as me, then you might sometimes think *you're* the issue. It's natural to question what's wrong with *you*, especially if you haven't met *the one* after X amount of dates. Let's not even go there with the comparison game because it doesn't do us any good.

President Theodore Roosevelt even said, "Comparison is the

thief of joy." And though I didn't know him personally, I think he was on to something. You have to remember that while your friends are getting engaged, married, or popping out babies left and right, that doesn't mean that's where you should be right now. You have to also remember, that doesn't mean they're happier or more successful than you. You have to remember to stay in your lane and that their timeline isn't the same as yours, and that's okay. Most importantly, I'm here to remind you that when it comes to men, remember darling, *it's them, not you.*

With all that being said, let's actually dive into the juicy details where I unpack different experiences with twelve men who made enough of an impression on me—both good and bad—to make it into this book.

THE ONE WHO TAUGHT ME EVERYTHING I SHOULDN'T DO ON A FIRST DATE

I WILL NOT USE THE REAL NAMES from my experiences in this book, so let's just refer to this first guy as Brooklyn. Brooklyn matched with me on December 5, 2018, at 10:48 a.m. He messaged me saying, "Hey gorgeous," with the heart eyes emoji. Now I will admit, he wasn't completely my type, but I thought *what the heck, what do I have to lose?* Again, I was completely open-minded when it came to online dating, so I wasn't too picky or shallow when it came to reviewing profiles.

At the time, I included the following prompt in my profile: *"the key to my heart is food and wine."* (Yes, I know, so basic and cliché, but this just confirms my newbie status when it came to online dating.) And not surprisingly, that's the one that Brooklyn decided to focus on in our initial conversation.

Brooklyn and I instantly converted from a few exchanges on the app to texting, which resulted in a proper date. Ladies, I'm talking about a full-on plan with dinner and drinks on a Friday night! For some strange reason, my mindset about first dates at that time was exactly how that night panned out. Looking back, I would *never* say yes to a dinner date, especially not on the first date. But keep in mind that I had been out of the dating game for quite some time, and I thought I wanted to be wined and dined, hence my not-so-creative prompt answer.

We decided to meet up at Jane on Houston Street, and I didn't know what to expect. I was a bit nervous only because this was my first official date with a complete stranger from a dating app. He arrived before I did. I spotted him at the bar, and I walked over to him and said hello. He was a bit shorter than I expected, and that was the first instance when I realized that men usually add an inch or two to their height on their profiles. I vividly remember I wore a black blouse that was off the shoulders to show my collar bones, and I thought it was a sexy but classy choice and paired it with black jeans and booties. This ensemble became my go-to first date outfit for my winter dates, and I wonder if any of you do the same? Brooklyn wore a black sweater and glasses, so he came off to me as a well put together man. I guess you can tell that we are both New Yorkers since we resorted to wearing black.

We were seated by the window, and it took me a while to get comfortable. When we were ordering food, I knew I had fucked up by agreeing to such a formal date. But I will give credit to Brooklyn, because he was a great conversationalist, and that made the experience less awkward. After downing a few drinks, I felt better about the situation and decided to just let things flow.

I actually ended up having a great time with Brooklyn because I forgot what it was like to be out with a guy. However, as the evening progressed, I started to realize that I didn't look at Brooklyn as a potential boyfriend or even see him as my date. Instead, I saw him as a companion that I was kicking with on a Friday night. We vibed well, and I was in such a great mood that I didn't want to go home just yet. After dinner, I could tell we were on the same page because he asked me what our next stop should be, and in that moment, I knew we would go wherever New York would take us.

Since we were in the Lower East Side, which is my stomping grounds, we decided to pay Pianos a visit. There's always a huge line there, and that night was no exception. I didn't know that Brooklyn was so well connected until we arrived, and we ended up bypassing the line because he knew the bouncer. I didn't tell him this, but I thought it was a smooth move on his part. If you live in NYC, you know how difficult it is for guys to get into a club/lounge if they don't have a hook up or if they aren't accompanied by a group of models. Needless to say, we danced the night away. I was drunk, and I was loving this single but ready to mingle phase. Our date was memorable and fun, and I felt like I found my inner college-version self coming out. The carefree spirit I had that evening gave me the confidence and excitement

I needed for the dating process.

Shortly after the first date, Brooklyn extended an invitation to cook dinner for me at his place. This was the second mistake I made in the early stages of online dating. I actually hate to call it a mistake since I learned from it, but I guess I would have done this differently knowing what I know today. When I arrived at his apartment located in Brooklyn (hence his reference name), I was pleasantly surprised by the space, the view, and the overall sophisticated vibe. It was definitely a place where I thought, *Damn, this is nice.*

I'm all about energy, and I wanted to be positive during that evening. I thought to myself that even though I didn't know how the date would go, I still had power in setting the tone through my energy and body language. I have no complaints about Brooklyn as an individual, and I truly believe he's a stand-up guy. He was successful, but beyond his success, he was motivated, grounded, and humble. He was an evident go-getter, and that drive was attractive to me.

I noticed he had flowers on his kitchen table. When I asked about them, he revealed that he gets flowers for himself and his mom every two weeks. Not only did I find this fact endearing and sweet, but it showed me that his decision to spruce up his apartment was for himself and not to impress anybody else. By bringing his mom into the picture, I could tell that he valued family, which is something I look for in a man.

However, if I'm going to be completely honest, I just wasn't feeling him in that romantic way, and I shouldn't have put myself in a situation where I knew going in could make me feel uncomfortable. I don't know if I was in denial about the reality of what was going on or if I was just open and excited about having another date. It's always an awkward situation when a man is clearly trying to pursue you when you don't feel that way about them.

And just to be clear, no, he wasn't aggressive in his advances, but I just mean gestures here and there like wanting a kiss, pulling me close and wanting to slow dance with me. His gestures would've been innocent and cute if I had actually wanted them, but again, I just wasn't feeling it. I mean cooking dinner is an intimate activity. Did I process that thought before? Nope. I was completely out of my logical thinking, and I truly did just go with the flow. Needless to say, I survived the evening and ended up going home afterward. I wasn't brave enough to express my feelings in person, and I definitely ignored my doubts. That date took place during the holidays, so I think we left the night with something along the lines of, "*Okay, so let me know what your New Year's plans are, and we can meet up!*"

We never met up or spoke afterward.

What I learned from that experience is that the first date should never be a dinner date. I know that seems so obvious, but I didn't think it was that odd at the time (and please remember, I am referencing this for women in their twenties who are meeting men from dating apps). I thought that's what real adults do and that's how dates should be, because that's what you basically see in movies. Those more experienced in dating will tell you that the first rule is to never commit yourself to a dinner. You have no idea how you and the other person will connect, if at all, and a dinner is just too much too soon. Grabbing a drink or a coffee instead takes the pressure off both parties, and that way you can do a quick meetup and leave if it doesn't go well. And if it does go well, you can take it further by grabbing a second drink or going somewhere else afterward.

I also learned that I wasn't comfortable speaking openly about my feelings, and that's totally my fault. I felt trapped when I was in Brooklyn's apartment, and I felt like I couldn't vocalize where my mind was at. I simply wanted to just enjoy the dinner and dive into meaningful conversations, rather than get close and physical (a first-base type of thing). I think my body language showed that I wasn't completely into it, but I didn't say it out loud, and I should've. And why is that? I know I'm not the only one that has been in that position before. Maybe it's because I lacked confidence, or maybe it's because I'm a natural people pleaser. Maybe it's because Brooklyn was the first man I went on a date with, or maybe it's because I was unfamiliar with how to act in a relationship. Whatever the reason, I learned from that experience that being vocal and not being ashamed of how I feel or putting the other person's feelings before myself is something I still need to work on to this day. I found this to be a recurring issue in my dating life after Brooklyn, but the beauty about dating is that you learn and grow as you continue to put yourself out there.

The thing about dating is that there's no rule book because we all have different experiences, and we all approach men and dates differently. While I've had people tell me about certain strategies and share advice that they have learned themselves or read from books, I was never the type to listen or follow them. This was my dating experience, after all, and it was not an easy decision to give online dating a try. I sat down and made the conscious decision to do so. I knew that if I was going to attempt online dating, I wanted to do it my way no matter what my mistakes or consequences would be. I've always been a huge advocate for taking risks and having my words and actions align with my values. I was going to remain true to that, even in dating.

I learned a lot from my dating journey, and each experience made it clearer to me what I'm looking for in a relationship and what my dating style is. I'm thankful for the short time I had with Brooklyn. Since then, I've never said yes to a dinner date as the first date, but then again, I don't think anybody offered that either. In terms of having dinner cooked for me, well that did happen, but you'll see with whom and how that turned out later.

KEY LESSONS

- DON'T SAY YES TO A DINNER DATE AS YOUR FIRST DATE.
- YOU HAVE A SAY IN WHAT TYPE OF DATE YOU WANT.
- SUPPRESSING YOUR THOUGHTS AND FEELINGS WON'T DO YOU OR YOUR DATE ANY GOOD.
- HONESTY IS THE BEST POLICY.

THE ONE WHO FULFILLED MY HIGH SCHOOL DESIRES

ONE OF MY OTHER earlier dating experiences was definitely an interesting one because it involved someone that I previously knew. I never thought about the possibility of matching with someone from my past, but my experience is further proof that although New York City is huge, it's also a small world in itself. I remember when I came across J, I did a second glance at his profile because he looked familiar. It didn't click right away where I knew him from. I just remember staring at his photos, and I thought to myself, *I know this guy, but I can't pinpoint from where.*

I initially didn't know what to do with J's profile, so I decided not to make any rash decisions in terms of whether or not I should match with him. When you come across a profile on Hinge, you can instantly heart it or X it, which is the same as swiping right or left. However, if you don't take any initial action, it actually remains in the pool of options until you make a decision whether or not you are interested in them. After a few days passed, it finally hit me where I knew J from. I used to work at a retail store that J managed. He's actually not that much older than me, so please don't think it was that weird older boss type of relationship.

The company was young and cool, and I started working there when I was in high school. I was seventeen years old at the time. I had a crush on J because he's a good-looking guy, but our interactions were minimal, as I would only see him in passing. So when I saw his profile, I thought that this would be a great opportunity to match with him and see where it goes. However, I tried to pretend that I wasn't aware of this fact, and I responded to one of his prompts in his profile about pizza, instead of referring to our past. He actually remembered me because his response said, "*Employees shouldn't be associated with managers.*"

But being the witty woman that I am, I convinced him to take a chance on me. After all, we were both older now, and I was a single woman in NYC. He clearly was also a single man in NYC, so it made sense for me to explore this with J. After a few exchanges, I wrote to him and said, "Take me out." I'm known to be a blunt woman, and if I want something, I'm going to get it. I've also learned that if you don't ask, you don't get, so ladies remember that the next time you're waiting for a guy to ask you out. We ended up grabbing drinks at Pegu on a Tuesday night at 9:30 p.m. Who the hell says yes to grabbing drinks on a weekday at 9:30 p.m. as a first date, you ask? Apparently, we agreed to that date, and we were the only souls at the bar that night.

I hadn't seen J since I went to college, so it'd been almost nine years. He was there before me and already had a drink in his hands. J looked pretty much the same, but he looked different in the sense that he seemed more mature. I was getting butterflies walking toward him, because I felt like I was meeting someone I knew, but a different version of him. I usually can be myself even with nerves, but with him, I don't even remember what the first words out of my mouth were. I'm not sure if he could tell that I was nervous, but he seemed to be the complete opposite and was very calm and comfortable. The night went smoothly since he was a familiar face and wasn't a complete stranger. Our conversation revolved around what we both had been up to since our working days, and it was like catching up with an old friend whom you secretly like.

With a few drinks in my system, my former feelings for him resurfaced, and I became head over heels (in a teenager type of way) for him. I don't know what it is about alcohol, but damn, she has a way of making us all feel good, doesn't she?

I have to admit, I got pretty drunk, and if I recall correctly, we actually took shots. Pickleback shots to be precise. I had no idea what the heck was in it at that time. But after researching it later on, I discovered that it's a whiskey shot followed by a shot of pickle juice. It honestly sounds so gross, come to think of it, but I do remember surprisingly enjoying the shots and asking myself why I hadn't known about them earlier. I would probably never do that with a stranger, but I felt a sense of comfort when I was with J. I was having a really good time with him, and I didn't want the night to end. As a drunk, twenty-seven year old, I was having the best night and one thing led to another. Before I knew it, we were in an Uber going to Hell's Kitchen, and I spent the night at his place. If you're wondering if we had sex, the short answer is yes. I'm not going to sugarcoat that, and I want to be as raw and honest about my experiences as possible. I enjoyed my night with J, and I want to emphasize that his body is unreal. He has abs of steel, and it was nice running my fingers on his chest and body. I bring this up because that's pretty much all I can remember from that evening. I left in the morning, and in a weird way, I didn't feel like I was doing a walk of shame. Since J and I knew each other, I felt like it was more of a reunion that took a turn instead. Afterward, J messaged me later that day on Hinge asking for my number because we hadn't exchanged numbers before that night.

I was happy to know that he wanted to see me again because I knew I was into him. We had a second date shortly after, and it was basically a repeat of what went down on the first date. Alcohol was involved and again, I had a great time with J. I was meeting one of my girlfriends the next day, and she could tell that something was up by the grin on my face. I've been told that when you've recently had sex, there's a different energy that you give off to the world, and she was not wrong. I felt like I was tapping into a different side of me—maybe a more promiscuous side, maybe a more daring side—either way, it was a side that I was ready to embrace and get to know.

Circling back to my time with J, after our second date, we had a short break since he went to see his family in Connecticut for the holidays. I was still into him and wanted to maintain an active conversation. I remember that we were texting, and I was basically hinting that I wanted to see him again after the holidays. He stopped texting me, but it wasn't instant or concerning. Our conversation wasn't one of those "quick texts back-and-forth" type of interaction. Instead, we messaged each other here and there, so I didn't find it unusual, especially since this was during Christmas break.

But after a few days passed, he never responded, and I just thought to myself, *Okay, whatever, that's that.* He ended up texting me over a week later to apologize for ghosting me, and he said that he didn't think we were a good match. I read that twice and didn't respond.

In hindsight, he was absolutely right. I don't think we even had any meaningful conversation; I don't think I knew much about him, and vice versa. The main reason why I was so infatuated with him was that we had a common ground of somewhat knowing each other. I think our past made us get along so well. When I was with him, I felt like I already knew him.

It's funny how the universe works. As I mentioned previously, I know that people enter our lives for a reason. In regards to J, I think he fulfilled my high school crush and desire for him. It was very innocent, and since nothing came of it then, it was time for the universe to allow that to happen nine years later. When

I think back to my experience with J, I learned that with dating, it's okay to have fun and to not put too much pressure on the other person or what the relationship really is. I think my ego was hurt a little when he said he didn't think we were a good match, because he was the first guy to say that to me since I started this whole online dating experience.

But the fact of the matter is, in the long run, we weren't meant to be anything serious anyways. We were meant to meet up, reminisce and have fun, and enjoy each other's company for that very short time span. I also think it's funny that he was one of my first dates on Hinge because the thought of connecting with someone from my past never dawned on me. The way I look at life is like a map: there are tons of people with their own paths, and when those paths cross, it doesn't mean it would be the end of them crossing again in the future.

Sometimes it's easier to believe that things in the past should stay in your past, but sometimes it's all about timing. Have you ever met someone and thought, *If we had met at a different time, we would be perfect together?* I know I've certainly had those thoughts! And I'm not saying in a different life, J and I would be together because I really don't believe that's the case. I just think my interaction with him shows that life works in strange ways and that you can enjoy something that's short lived. I can appreciate the experience and not be upset that it didn't turn into anything more.

KEY LESSONS

- THE PAST DOESN'T ALWAYS STAY IN THE PAST.
- IT'S OKAY TO HAVE FUN ON YOUR DATES!
- DON'T PUT TOO MUCH PRESSURE ON YOURSELF AND WHAT YOU THINK YOUR RELATIONSHIP SHOULD BE, ESPECIALLY IN THE BEGINNING STAGES OF DATING.

THE ONE WHO SERENADED ME

I KNEW EARLY ON that I was a fan of witty banter because I had one of the most memorable conversations on the app with a guy who had "astronaut" listed as his occupation. I thought to myself, *There's no way that he's actually an astronaut*. But I thought it was funny, and I was intrigued to know more. I wanted to lean into it and see what kind of response I would get from this interaction.

Hinge has this compatibility feature, which says, *"Based on your hinge activity, we believe you have the best chance for a great first date. We found that, on average, you're 8x more likely to go on a date with your Most Compatible than you are with any other Hinge member."*

That was the first time I came across that note. And this time, I was doing the swiping, so I decided to like a video from this astronaut's profile of him playing the piano. (As I write this, the image of an actual person in an astronaut suit sitting down playing a piano is hilarious to me, and I thought I'd point that visual out for you as well.) Our initial conversation occurred on January 23, 2019. It was very sarcastic, but I thought, *Wow, this guy actually gets my humor.* I'm going to include the whole conversation below, so you can understand exactly what I'm referring to when I say witty banter:

Him: "You are quite the sharpshooter, huh?" *(referring to a video of me shooting hoops in an arcade game on my profile)*

Me: "I try."

Him: "Any other hidden talents?"

Me: "I can eat an endless amount of sushi."

Him: "Oh, that's where I know you from. There's a photo of you hanging at the front of the all-you-can-eat-sushi joint by my apartment."

Me: "Oh damn, they still have it up?"

Him: "They say you cleaned them out. They almost went bankrupt."

Me: "Hmm . . . so I guess it's time to find a new sushi spot. Any recommendations?"

Him: "I might. You asking me out?"

Me: "I was hoping you'd ask me out."

Him: "Okay, but fair warning, I haven't made a billion dollars yet, so I don't think I can take you out for sushi."

Me: "What billion-dollar sushi place do you know of? I was thinking something more low key and casual."

Him: "Well, if you can eat unlimited amounts, then it doesn't matter what place it is. But low key and causal sounds nice. Give me your number, and we'll set that up."

Me: "I have one issue."

Him: "Just one?"

Me: "Actually many. But one current."

Him: "Okay, at least you've got your issues prioritized. Go on."

Me: "It's my birthday weekend, and I'm leaving to visit Iceland on Monday."

Him: "Does that mean now or never?"

Me: "Well, I'm not moving to Iceland. But it's either sometime this weekend or next weekend."

Him: "Okay, I hope to make it so you don't miss me too much."

Me: "I hope you don't find another person who can eat more sushi than me."

Him: "Impossible, you're one of a kind."

Me: "No, I think you're one of a kind. I mean, apparently, you know how to play the piano, you're a pro at backflips, you can dance, and you also work as an astronaut, but that's pretty hard to believe."

Him: "Dreams do come true."

Me: "So you've been to the moon."

Him: "Yeah, I'll fly you there; we'll dance among the stars."

Me: "Wow, that's my dream date."

Him: "Enter your number in the text box below for a chance to win."

Me: "XXX-XXX-XXX *Fingers crossed, I hope I win."

Him: "Your application will be given the utmost consideration."

Even recalling our conversation makes me gush and laugh out loud because this was the type of unrealistic but comforting conversation that I was looking for. He ended up texting me on January 25th, and I remember this clearly because my birthday is on the 27th, which fell on a Sunday. I told him that our options of meeting up were limited because I was celebrating my birthday with my girlfriends the next day, and I was also leaving for Iceland for a week two days after. I wasn't sure how we were going to make this happen. Sure, we could've waited until I was back, but I know whenever there is too much time between talking to someone and actually meeting them in person, it usually doesn't work out.

It was my golden birthday, and I had everything planned out. For those of you who don't know what that is, a golden birthday is the year you turn the same age as your birthday (so I was turning 27 on the 27th).

I had a hotel booked for the night so all my friends could meet me there, and Rochelle (one of my best friends) could spend the night since she lives in Philly. I was going to spend the day with her, and then we were going to get ready and pregame at the hotel with my other friends before heading to dinner at the hotel's restaurant. All of us were then going to grab drinks at a lounge next door before going out afterward. (If you can't tell, yes, I'm the planner in the group.) The only scenario I could think of was if Astronaut met me at the lounge for a speed date, and he agreed.

Mind you, I was with six of my girlfriends, and it was the funniest "first date" encounter ever. He basically met me at the bar while all my friends were somewhere in the corner, pretty much spying on us discreetly and watching this whole thing go down. I don't remember what we talked about, but our conversation lasted for about twenty-five minutes before I said "peace out" because I was about to party the night away.

Needless to say, Astronaut and I still kept in touch, and we had a proper first date after I came back from Iceland. We met at some midtown bar and grabbed some drinks, and then we got to know each other without distractions that time. My initial impression of him was that he was a gentleman. He was older, I think thirty-four years old at the time. He was six foot one and just carried himself in a way that I respected. I also don't know what it was about him, but every time I walked with him, he always made me feel safe and that I had nothing to worry about.

We went back to his place that night, but I knew that nothing was going to go down. He lived in midtown, and his place was nice. I mean, he could've worked on his interior design skills, but given that he's a guy, I decided to cut him some slack. The first thing I noticed was the piano in the living room, which definitely piqued my interest. The only song I know how to play is "Mary Had a Little Lamb," so I decided to show off my skills. Little did I know, this guy didn't have the piano just for show. He was actually an experienced and skilled piano player and told me that he took lessons growing up in Russia.

He started to play some songs, and I was impressed by the

fact that he didn't even need to look at the sheets of music to figure out which notes to play. He then asked what I wanted to hear, and I soon realized that he could basically play any song without looking it up. One of my favorite songs of all time is "A Whole New World" from *Aladdin*. He started to play the beginning of the song, and then out of nowhere, he started to sing. I thought, *What the fuck is going on*! He actually sings really well and has a beautiful voice.

I was not expecting any of this to happen, and I had no idea how to react. But I must admit, during this private concert, my panties were about to come off (not literally, but you ladies know what I mean). I was honestly getting so turned on because, for a quick second, I was looking at the scenario from an outsider's point of view. *I just met a man who is not only charming, witty, and successful in his career, but he also knows how to play the piano and can sing. He is serenading me in his NYC apartment, overlooking the skyscrapers on this cold but cozy, beautiful Friday night. Am I dreaming? How is this happening right now?*

I turned to him and thought to myself, *If this is his plan to make me fall in love, then it's going to work.* I remember even telling him that he can't just pull these moves out of nowhere because ladies will fall for this. Needless to say, I enjoyed my evening with him and took advantage of my private one-on-one concert. I remember there was a moment, however, where we kissed and his advances toward me made me pull back. He got comfortable with being close to me and was getting a little too touchy. I just wasn't ready for that, and I didn't think he was insinuating sex, but I still didn't want us to go that far. I don't think I said anything out loud, but my body language showed that I wasn't 100 percent into it. I then told him I was going to head home and ordered an Uber afterward.

I'm a "go with the flow" type of gal, and I will say this over and over again. Everything about that night was perfect. I really liked how things were progressing, but I still felt like I didn't know this guy since it was only our first official date. Yes, we kissed here and there, but I didn't feel like I needed to submit to being touched in places that I wasn't comfortable with, just yet. But for the record, the night didn't leave me with a sour taste, and I still wanted to get to know more about this mysterious, talented man. I also learned later that I'm more on the reserved side when it comes to affection, and I like to take things slowly until I'm comfortable with the guy and can see that the relationship is going somewhere.

Our second and third dates took place at a sushi restaurant. Yes, there will be tons of sushi mentions in this book because I love sushi. I also think it's important for men to know my interests and take note of them. Besides, it was a running joke considering our initial conversation regarding sushi. After we had dinner, we decided to go to Fat Cat in the West Village. I'm embarrassed to say as a native New Yorker, I'd actually never been there before, so I was excited, to say the least. I knew that it was a cool bar that offers live music, pool, ping-pong, and board games, and that's the vibe that we were looking for. We put our names down to play ping-pong, but we realized shortly that we would not be able to play that night since the waitlist was ridiculously long.

We settled for playing Scrabble instead, ordered some beer, and sat at a corner. Our date was such a fun experience, and I highly recommend doing activities if you want something different than just a drink at a bar. I'm a competitive player, but I pretended that I wasn't. I really wanted to win at Scrabble, but I was underestimating Astronaut's wide range of vocabulary because I was losing by a landslide. I took note of all the big words that Astronaut played that night, and I was attracted to his intellect. After we played two games, we called it a night.

I saw Astronaut one more time after that, but our final date was a bit blurry (not due to alcohol but due to my lack of memory). I think it was a repeat of the second and third dates. We probably grabbed some dinner and drinks before heading back to his place. He played the piano for me again, and I really enjoyed it. We cuddled a little on his couch afterward, but again, he began to touch me and attempted to take off my bra. That's when I decided we were not going any further with our date. I got myself together, and I told him that I wasn't ready for that. He said he understood. He also mentioned that he really liked me and that's his way of showing it, and he didn't see anything wrong with what he was doing given the fact that we were both looking to date.

I can understand where he was coming from, but I just felt like he wasn't listening and taking in what I was saying. Once I figured out that we weren't on the same page, I ended up going home, and I don't think Astronaut and I spoke after that.

And I know some of you might seem confused because I had no issues going home with J, so why was I making such a big deal with Astronaut? I will warn you that my actions aren't very consistent, as you'll see from the other dates I will mention later on. The only conclusion or explanation I can come up with is that I'm a feeler, and I go by whatever I feel in the moment. Sometimes, I surrender to attraction and my hormones, and sometimes, if I actually see potential in someone or in a relationship, I take a step back, and I'm more reserved. I know some of you are nodding your head, because I can't be the only one who operates this way, right?

What I learned from my date and experience with Astronaut is that it's okay to walk away, even if you have a good thing in front of you, if the person can't respect your comfort level and your boundaries. Looking back, I was actually really fond of him, and I think if he took a step back and took things at a slower pace like I wanted, we could've had something special. He wasn't a bad guy. I don't think he had any bad intentions, but his approach to dating was just different from mine. I also learned that I was still shy, and I still wasn't comfortable standing my ground.

I mentioned the word *boundaries* in this chapter, but I didn't put too much weight on that concept until much later into my dating journey. I was still scared to say how I felt and wasn't honoring or validating my feelings. I still had this weird inclination of having to please the other person. I think my need to please others stems from my natural habit of wanting everybody to like me and the fact that I was still figuring out my personal dating style, but this experience would soon shape me to become a more confident dater and communicator down the road.

It's actually so interesting to go down memory lane because I can look at myself two years ago through a fresh, more mature lens. Although I was twenty-six at the time and very much an adult, I was still a baby when it came to the NYC dating scene. While I was dedicating time to getting to know these men and putting myself out there, I didn't know that I was also learning more about myself and navigating all that comes with being a single woman living in New York. Yes, dating is a lot of fun, but it can also be overwhelming. And sometimes, you do have to take a step back and figure out your boundaries and dealbreakers before diving headfirst into these dates.

With all that being said, I was still back in the game and was open to who else was coming my way next.

KEY LESSONS

- VIBES DON'T LIE.
- A GUY SHOULD ALWAYS RESPECT YOUR BOUNDARIES.
- YOU CAN WALK AWAY FROM SOMEONE GOOD IF THEY MAKE YOU FEEL UNCOMFORTABLE.
- YOU HAVE EVERY RIGHT TO VALIDATE AND HONOR YOUR OWN FEELINGS.

THE ONE WHO I
SHOULD'VE FUCKED

I HADN'T CHANGED any of my photos or prompts on the app, and from first glance, it was obvious that I loved food and wine. As I reflect on the information and prompts I chose when I first created my profile, it was clear that I was a newbie with online dating. I have concluded that when someone has basic information on the app, it's either they are not good at pitching themselves because they don't really know how to use the prompts to showcase their strengths, or they're just a surface level individual. A good way to judge your own profile is to also see it from the receiver's end. I find profiles that are filled to capacity more appealing than those that are empty. I can appreciate those who put the effort into their profile because it's a reflection of what they're looking for.

But anyway, back to my dating stories. I will now introduce you to Mr. Chef. As his name suggests, yes, Mr. Chef was actually a chef. When we matched, I did a double take because this guy was handsome and completely my type! I am usually more drawn to guys with darker features who are on the taller side and have a nice smile and inviting eyes. Our initial conversation obviously revolved around food, and he teased me by saying that he would cook for me. I received this offer differently than I did with Brooklyn because he was the real deal.

I remember clearly in the beginning stages of our relationship, something odd happened (it's not so odd now, but I remember thinking it was so strange at the time). When we were about to take things offline, he asked for my Instagram handle, but I offered to give him my number instead. For those who are confused about my response, let me explain where my mind is when it comes to social media. I totally understand why guys want an Instagram profile. They want to see more photos of the girl to validate their profile and appearance. However, since I have a social media presence, and it's a huge part of my job, I was skeptical to give that information because I feared that guys would judge me before getting to know me. I also have tons of information on my profile—dating back years and years—and I would rather have someone get to know me and find those details out from me, rather than from social media.

Mr. Chef came back with a response that basically said, "I think a number is too soon. Can we chat on Instagram?" I thought that was so weird, and I brought this up to one of my girlfriends who also thought it was strange. In my mind, I thought the more appropriate route would be to ask for my Instagram after a few back-and-forth exchanges. It took me a few days to decide what to do, but he was so attractive that I was like fuck it, he can have my Instagram. I gave it to him, and we instantly chatted through direct messaging. He apologized for asking and explained that he didn't want to be catfished, which I understood. I then explained my hesitancy with giving my account to him, and he understood where I came from. Now that we were both on the same page, we ditched talking through direct messaging and finally graduated to texting.

Oh, I also forgot to mention that Mr. Chef lived in Jersey. Of course, that's not an ideal location, but he drove, so I didn't care. And again, I wasn't looking that far into the future with this guy. He was a chef at an Upper East Side restaurant, so he frequently traveled to the city. Our first date took place at Bar Veloce located in the East Village. They are notable for a good wine selection, and my profile screamed that I love wine, so that's the place we agreed on.

He texted me about twenty minutes earlier than we were supposed to meet. His message said that he was already at the bar but to take my time. After reading his message, I decided not to rush and arrived at the time we initially agreed on. Also, on a side note, I often don't like to be the first one at a bar, especially on a first date. I always feel awkward waiting for a stranger to show up, so I always try to show up about five to ten minutes later, but never more than fifteen. When I first entered, I was excited because not only was Mr. Chef attractive, but we also had good conversations prior to meeting up. The evening was going well, and we shared a strong chemistry.

I found Mr. Chef to be so interesting because I had never met a chef before. On first dates, I find myself asking a lot of the questions because I love getting to know someone. I also know that most people like hearing themselves speak, so I allowed Mr. Chef the stage to tell me about his love for food and what it was like living his dream job. It makes me happy when people talk about things they are passionate about because you can tell from their body language that they love what they do. And it was clear that Mr. Chef loved what he did.

As the night progressed, Mr. Chef was very responsible in managing our alcohol, and I actually didn't get drunk this time! (I'd like to disclose that I'm not a huge drinker. I just get easily drunk because I'm a lightweight thanks to my genes.)

Mr. Chef had to work early at the restaurant the next day, so I believe we had maybe two glasses of wine paired with some delicious cheese. It was the perfect amount for me.

We planned that he would cook for me on the second date, and I was willing to make the trip to New Jersey. While I was figuring out the transportation, Mr. Chef realized it might be easier if I just took the train to the Upper East Side, and he would pick me up, as that was similar to him driving to the city for work. So we did that on a weekend, but while we were driving to his place, he mentioned there was a Japanese market along the way, and I almost lost my shit.

I like to think I'm well traveled, and Japan is by far one of my favorite places in the world. Japanese cuisine is on the top of my food list, so we scratched the cooking plan and decided to go to the market to get some goodies instead. There were so many options to choose from, and I was in food heaven. After touring the place and visiting all the different vendors, we chose sushi, ice cream, and chocolate, the best combination for a meal, in my opinion.

When I arrived at his place, I saw his kitchen first after entering through the front door, and I was mesmerized. His kitchen could've been featured in a magazine or as an after-renovation photo from one of those HGTV shows. It wasn't big by any means, but the size was perfect. It was white, clean, and bright, and there were accents of navy blue here and there. There were tons of kitchen utensils and cookware. I don't know much about brands, but I could tell they were all high quality. Needless to say, I was in love.

We brought the food to the living room, and we ended up watching a movie that I can't recall. Let's be honest, when it comes to dating, the movie isn't the focus—it's the other person. We ate and cuddled after, but it was all very innocent. I also appreciated that Mr. Chef didn't make me feel uncomfortable as some men have. We both understood that this was a second date in his apartment, but there were no intentions of being physically intimate. After the movie, I ended up calling an Uber home and overall felt good about where our relationship could potentially go.

I remember our third date happened toward the end of

February because I had a pre-Oscars viewing party to attend, which just so happened to fall on his birthday. I think he had plans and so did I, so we weren't planning on seeing each other that day. When I was at my viewing party, I received a text message from him around 5:30 p.m. He told me that his plans had ended early, and he knew I was busy, but if I wanted to, I could go over to his place to watch the Oscars with him.

If it were anybody else, I wouldn't have said yes since he lived all the way in Jersey, and it was a last-minute thing. I had to think about his offer, but I thought, *fuck it*. I was already glammed up, and I did have some time to go home, change into my regular clothes, and head over since the ride was only thirty minutes. I spoke to some of my friends at the party, and they all encouraged me to go, so that was the only push and encouragement I needed.

I rushed home to change, and I ended up picking up some pastries from Supermoon Bakehouse because I didn't want to show up empty-handed. I took an Uber to his place, and I think I got there right before the Oscars broadcast was airing at 8 p.m. He was pleasantly surprised that I brought him some desserts. I wanted to show him that I liked him, and since it was his birthday, I wanted to make him feel special.

I don't think Mr. Chef actually cared about the Oscars and quite frankly I didn't either, but it was nice to watch the Oscars with him since it didn't require much focus as it's an awards show. We enjoyed each other's company, and I could feel the sexual tension between us. Going into the date, I didn't think anything of it, and while I was there, I don't think I would've minded if we had sex. However, I liked that we were both on the same page because he did mention something about wanting to do "things" to me but knew he shouldn't.

From the title of the chapter, you can already guess that we didn't have sex, but looking back, we should have. Why? Because clearly, I didn't get that opportunity, and it has left me to wonder what that experience would've been like.

When the Oscars ended, I went home, and we continued to talk. We had a great time getting to know each other in the following weeks. I was invited to the Hudson Yards opening, and I invited him as my guest because the restaurant and culinary scene was a huge part of Hudson Yard's offerings and marketing. I naturally thought of Mr. Chef, and I figured it would be a fun and appropriate event to experience together, considering his passion and love for food and what he does for a living.

But a week before the event, I received a text message that he needed to tell me something, and we all know that's never a good sign. He called me to let me know that he received a job offer to work as the main chef in a restaurant opening in Hawaii. He wasn't sure if he was going to take the job, but it would obviously affect our relationship. I was relieved that it was something to do with his career rather than me. I assured him that he needed to make the best decision for himself, without considering me, because we weren't even that serious at the time.

We ended on a good note, and we were on the same page. I appreciate that he kept me in the loop about the offer. In the days leading up to the Hudson Yards opening event, he basically told me that he was planning to take the job offer and maybe it wouldn't be a good idea to go to the event as my date, but that he was still attending. I thought that was very strange because I was the one who invited him to the event. Isn't it common sense that if he decides not to go with me, that he shouldn't go at all? I guess in his defense, he had a friend who was also invited. So I'm assuming in his mind, he reasoned it out that he would've been at the event regardless. Still, the way that panned out didn't really sit well with me.

However, I didn't care at this point because I was going to the event no matter what, and I had friends attending as well. We did agree that when we were there, we would say hi to each other. Since it was the opening night, I didn't know how big the turnout would be. Hudson Yards is massive, and there were so many people everywhere that it was a full house that evening.

After touring the space and restaurants for a while, I texted him asking if he was there, and he answered yes. He told me where he was, but after a while, I thought, *What's the point of even going to see him.* I already knew that nothing would come out of it. Plus, it was such a chaotic event, that I didn't think it was worth my time to maneuver through all the crowds just to find him and say hi. Instead, I just thought to myself, *If I bump into him, that's cool, and if I don't, that's cool too.* I ended up enjoying the evening with my friends, and that was the end of Mr. Chef.

I recall this experience because this relationship took a turn. Things started out well with Mr. Chef, and I liked that we were on the same page. We didn't rush into anything, and we actually spent time getting to know each other. What's unique about this relationship is how it ended. Neither one of us expected that he would get a job offer in Hawaii. He wasn't even looking for a job, but the job offer fell in his lap. To this day, I have no idea if he actually took it or what he's up to right now.

This is proof of why I truly believe in the power of timing. Had Mr. Chef and I met at a later time or a different time, who knows if we would've ended up together. Love is complicated and rare, but it's not impossible. When love works, it's magical, because everything else has to align. Not only do two people have to be attracted to each other and be compatible and have similar values and interests, but they also need to be on the same page in terms of where their lives are heading. Remember when I referenced the map visual earlier? In this case, my life path was heading toward one direction, and his life path was heading in the total opposite direction. There was no way for us to have worked out, and that's why it's such a beautiful occurrence when you find the right one.

This experience also made it clear to me that you should just go with your gut and honor how you feel. If you try to plan for the future or live by some dating rules, then you can't truly be present in the moment and enjoy what's in front of you. By this point, I started to be optimistic about this dating process, although I hadn't found the one yet. It was just fascinating for me to meet new people, and I was hopeful to see who else I would come across.

KEY LESSONS

- TIMING IS EVERYTHING IN A RELATIONSHIP.
- BE PRESENT ON YOUR DATES AND DON'T PLAN TOO MUCH FOR THE FUTURE, BECAUSE YOU NEVER KNOW HOW THE RELATIONSHIP WILL END.
- MAKE YOUR OWN RULES FOR DATING.

5

THE ONE WHO SHARED OUR FIRST
DATE WITH ALL MY FRIENDS

EVEN IF WE DON'T UNDERSTAND it at the time, we are meant to meet certain people in our lives, and we can look back and laugh and be grateful that we've had those encounters. This is how I feel about Ducati. My memories of Ducati aren't extremely clear since we only had four dates that took place over the course of three weeks, but I will say that our dates were the most unique dates I've ever been on.

Ducati had these gorgeous green-hazel eyes, which is what made me match with him despite him being five feet eight inches tall. Ducati liked one of my videos on my Hinge profile on April 17, 2019. He messaged me and said, "Hi, how's it going :)." Our conversation was very light, and he mentioned that he was looking for someone with no drama. He asked if I wanted to give this a try. I thought his response was cute, and I felt good, laid-back vibes from him.

During the month of April, I was actually doing the Whole30 diet, so I was up-front about this. I said that my only request would be no alcohol when we met up, and he followed up by asking if any food was allowed.

I wrote back the following: "I have a list of approved foods, lol, but I can still have fish, chicken, brown rice, and sweet potatoes, so probably Mediterranean cuisine."

Looking back, I can't help but laugh out loud because I'm not sure what guy would've still been interested in meeting me with all these specific diet restrictions, but Ducati was. He didn't make any judgments or comments about my health choice. And from that moment on, I knew that he was different and probably one of the rare "good guys." We exchanged numbers shortly after.

I was going to a Yankees baseball game the following night with seven of my friends, but one of my friends couldn't make it last minute. I remember getting the message from her as I was about to get on the F train on Delancey Street. It just so happens that I was also texting Ducati at that time, and a weird thought came to mind. *What if I invited him to the baseball game?*

I pondered that idea for a moment, and I texted a few of my girlfriends who were attending the game to ask if that was weird. They said, "Maybe a little, but who cares." I could extend the invitation, and whether or not he accepts it is up to him. I didn't want the ticket to go to waste, and I didn't think he would come. I took a chance and told him that I was heading to a Yankees game and that I had an extra ticket. I mentioned that he was welcome to come if he didn't have any plans, but seven of my other friends were joining too (five of whom were girls and two were guys). Surprisingly, he said yes, and this is why Ducati is known as the one who shared our first date with all my friends.

I was excited for the game because I thought this night could go horribly bad or extremely well. Either way, I was okay with the outcome because I knew that this would go down as one of the most hilarious moments of my life. I mean, let's all take a moment to digest the situation. I had just matched with this random guy on Hinge, and we had exchanged numbers the previous night. Less than twenty-four hours later, I was now inviting him to a baseball game with my friends. I mean, what could go wrong?

I transferred to the D train on 34th street and was making my way to the stadium. I met all my friends in front of the gates, and we headed inside. I also gave them a heads-up that my date would be joining us, and I guess they were all excited for this Thursday night spectacle.

Ducati texted me saying that he was on his way. My friends and I were already at our seats when he texted me saying that he couldn't get in because he had a laptop since he was coming straight from work. I felt horrible because I knew that the trip from midtown wasn't easy, but he was confident that he would find a way to get in. He reacted calmly, and his behavior showed me his good nature and that he was a problem solver.

He mentioned that he found a place where he could store it in a locker. I didn't even know they had lockers near Yankees

Stadium but hey, *whatever works*, I thought to myself. I'm not sure how he managed to get through security so quickly, but ten minutes later, he texted me saying that he was inside and was making his way to our section.

I saw him approaching us, and he was wearing his backpack and a dark blue flannel shirt with a black vest. I saved a seat for him next to mine and said hello. The first thing I noticed was his deep voice. We broke the ice by having him introduce himself to my friends, and then I asked him about the laptop situation. He told me that he ended up camouflaging it in his backpack when they searched it the second time, and he was able to get in with no issue. I didn't even think about what he said at that moment, but as I recall this incident now, I can't help but laugh because it was so random, and I find random shit funny.

We ended up talking for a few minutes before we got food and drinks for the group, as that was the only "alone" time we had. He was also a gentleman because he kindly offered to pay for my friends' drinks and food that night. The rest of the evening went smoothly as we spoke casually while watching the game. When it was over, we all took the train back, and he made conversation with my male friends. I thought he was such a good sport for not only saying yes to this first group date but also making the most of the situation. I don't think I could've done what he did had the roles been reversed.

Shortly after the game, Ducati and I set up a one-on-one date for that Saturday. He is referenced here as "Ducati" because he's a motorcycle lover, and one of his Hinge photos showed him on a motorcycle. During the Yankees game, he actually told me that he was shopping for a new motorcycle when I asked what his weekend plans were. I didn't have plans for the weekend because I was single as fuck, so I told him that I would be down to go with him if he wanted some company. I remember that he was taken aback by my response because he didn't think a girl would be interested in that. I reminded him that I love doing things that are out of the ordinary, and it sounded like an adventure. He took me up on that offer, and that's how I spent my Saturday afternoon—at a motorcycle dealership.

It was such a cool experience, and I loved seeing how excited he was to find his new baby. I was definitely the odd one out at the dealership, because I don't ride motorcycles, and I don't know anything about them. The environment didn't make me feel uncomfortable or awkward, because I was there to accompany Ducati and it was a situation that I was willing to embrace.

We visited Harley Davidson afterward, and this is where he tested one of their motorcycles. I will say that it was attractive to see him riding one because a man on a motorcycle just screams badass to me. I wasn't sure how I felt about dating or being with a guy who rode motorcycles, since I know they're dangerous, but I wasn't thinking about that at the time. I just went with the flow as I normally did, and I learned a lot about motorcycles that afternoon.

After we looked at the different bikes, we decided to grab some food. Due to my dietary restrictions, he mentioned that there was an authentic fish market/restaurant in Queens, but it wasn't fancy by any means. He explained the concept. You pick out your fish like you would in a fish market. Then they cook it for you and bring it to your table for you to enjoy. This experience was as local as it gets, and you are served with paper plates and utensils. I jumped at that idea because I love authentic places. I'm really not into fancy restaurants, and I'm always down to get out of my comfort zone. I also rarely venture out to Queens, so this was a good opportunity to do so. (All my New Yorkers can attest that we often stay within the borough we reside in, and we each have our own limitations on how far we'll travel.)

We drove to Astoria Seafood, and there was already a line when we arrived. We probably waited close to forty-five minutes, but it was fine since we had each other to converse with. The environment of the restaurant was so chaotic, and all I saw were people talking loudly. There were conversations blending into each other with random bursts of laughter and jokes. I'm not sure how many other women would've been okay with this scene, considering it was technically our first date, but I was here for it.

Once they called our names, we went inside and chose our fish. I think we basically selected one of everything, including sardines, snappers, salmon, and branzino. We also ordered potatoes and Greek salad to share. When the food came, it was like Thanksgiving, and we were feasting. I figured since we were already in this type of restaurant, there was no point in trying to look classy or cute, and I should just eat this food as it was made to be enjoyed. Did this break the Whole30 rules? Probably. But was it worth it? You bet.

The fish was hands down one of the best fish dishes I've had in New York, and it comes close to the amazing fish I had in Portugal. I remember that I even sent a photo to my mom raving about the place, and I told her that we should go there one day.

After we finished eating, Ducati drove me home. I had a great time with him, and I loved that it was so different from the several dates I'd had before. To this day, it still ranks as one of the most memorable dates that I've been on. What I found so special about Ducati was that he wasn't like the rest of the guys on the app. He was comfortable with himself and had no problem vocalizing his interests. I didn't feel pressured to act a certain way, either. During that first date, we were both ourselves, and there wasn't any judgment from either side.

We went on two more dates after that. On the third date, we went to a Japanese restaurant near where he lived, and then we drove to Coney Island afterward. We decided to take a quick stroll on the boardwalk, right by the beach, even though it was a chilly night in April. He was holding me close. And as I was hugging him with my arms around his waist, I remember thinking that we were having such a romantic moment. I felt a sense of emptiness creep in because I wasn't enjoying it as much as I should have. I realized that, when it came down to it, I didn't have any romantic feelings for Ducati. While I enjoyed hanging out with him, I couldn't get myself to feel for him in that way, so it was difficult for me to give in.

Our fourth date was also our last date. We ended up grabbing dinner at Baby Brasa. At this point, I already knew that I didn't see a future with him, and it was clear because there wasn't a strong connection that night. A part of me felt bad because I knew that he drove all the way to the West Village from Brooklyn only to have an hour-long dinner with me, but then again, this is what you have to do when it comes to dating. You have to put yourself out there and just see where it goes.

I wasn't brave enough to be transparent with my feelings that night because I was still going back-and-forth about him. After all, he was just a good guy, and I knew he didn't do anything wrong. As you can all see, there was a pattern that was forming. I was finding myself in similar situations of not feeling comfortable vocalizing my feelings with different guys. I really wanted to make things work with Ducati, but at the end of the day, love can't be forced. I think he could tell that I wasn't 100 percent present or into it. But he was still such a gentleman and told me that if I wanted to end the night early, then he would drive me home, and that's what we did.

He texted me a few days later with a simple "Hi." After marinating with my feelings, I finally decided that there was no point in giving us another go, and it was time to pull the cord. I put on my big girl pants and sent him a message explaining how I felt. Ducati was the first guy that I had messaged to end things with. I don't remember my exact words but it was something along the lines of how I enjoyed his company, but that I didn't see a future with him. He didn't respond, and I don't blame him because I'm not sure what he could've said to change the situation or if he needed to say anything anyways.

Ducati was a unique man, and I am grateful that he came into my life because he showed me that when it comes to dating, you don't have to follow the cliché dates route. Sometimes the best stories and experiences are the ones where you just say yes and don't question. There wasn't a doubt or hesitation in his mind when he decided to meet me at Yankees stadium that night. He didn't question who was going to be there. He basically went into that experience blindly, but with the mentality that he was going to have a good time.

I also learned that there are good quality guys out there, but you also can't force connections, chemistry, or feelings. While I do believe that feelings can be formed later, there still needs to be a strong connection at the beginning for the spark to reveal itself. I was waiting for the spark to appear, but it never did. And that's okay. I learned that whatever doesn't heal from past relationships will manifest in current and future ones. It's the universe's way of teaching us a lesson by having us experience it over and over again until we take action and break the cycle or change the narrative.

I still have faith in love, but I'm reminded time and time again that it's actually rare. When I was young, I used to think that love was easy and that I would find a man with no issue. Growing up, whenever the commercials would come on for *The Bachelor* on ABC, I would think to myself, *Why are these beautiful "older" women going on a dating reality competition show to find love?* I never understood why these women were single in the first place. And a decade later, it all makes sense to me, which is why I am now a *Bachelor/Bachelorette* fanatic. Now that I'm getting older, I have realized that there are tons of factors that play into a relationship, and for it to work out, the formula needs to be right. Compatibility and attraction are just the initial variables. You then need to factor in timing, values, interests, etc.

Ducati wasn't my person. I'm sure he would be perfect for someone else, but when Hinge matched us, he wasn't the value of my X. But I would soon learn that I would find someone that would complete my equation (at least temporarily).

KEY LESSONS

- YOU CAN'T FORCE A CONNECTION IF IT JUST ISN'T THERE.
- BE SPONTANEOUS, SAY YES, AND GET OUT OF YOUR COMFORT ZONES WHEN IT COMES TO DATING.
- SOMETIMES, WE HAVE TO END RELATIONSHIPS WITH GOOD PEOPLE EVEN WHEN IT'S NOT AN EASY TO DECISION TO MAKE.

THE ONE WHO MADE ME LIKE OLDER MEN

ALL MY GIRLFRIENDS know that I have a thing for older men. I don't know if it's because most of the guys I've interacted with in the past were just immature, but I have this theory that some might call silly. I believe if a guy is my age, or even a few years older than me, that we just wouldn't be a good fit because his maturity level is just not on par with mine. And come to think of it, I prefer someone to be even more mature than I am because I want to be challenged, and I'm really drawn to intellectual conversations and growth-oriented individuals.

When I first downloaded Hinge, I discovered that you can set your preferences, including height, age, religion, political views, family plans, etc. Since I wanted to go for older men, I think I initially had my age range from thirty-two to thirty-eight. The oldest guy I've ever had a connection with in my past was eight years older than me, so I thought ten years would be a good starting limit. I also think it's totally okay to have preferences when it comes to dating, and I would just be cautious about putting too many restrictions on your dating life.

Needless to say, I have been curious to see if there was any validity in my attraction for older men, which led me to do an online search of articles. A study[1] that was published in the academic journal *Cerebral Cortex* in 2013 states that, "the female brain establishes connections and prunes itself faster than the male brain." This study basically confirms there is scientific proof that supports my theory that it takes more time for males to form their maturity compared to women. I think that's also why some men don't act their age and why I've been a bit turned off by younger men. So, I'd be the first to openly admit that I rarely give younger men the time of day. For me, maturity is attractive, so I tend to associate older men with higher levels of maturity. I do want to also add that maturity and playfulness are not the same. I like a man who is mature enough to hold serious conversations but also would be down to act a fool every now and then and join me in my silliness.

Since I was looking for something more on the serious side by this point, I figured that older men would have similar values in finding something more sustainable, assuming they got their

---

[1] "Preferential Detachment During Human Brain Development: Age- and Sex-Specific Structural Connectivity in Diffusion Tensor Imaging (DTI) Data," *Cerebral Cortex*, 15 December 2013, https://academic.oup.com/cercor/article/25/6/1477/299218

fuckboy tendencies out of their system earlier on. I also knew I was looking for someone who had their shit together and knew what they wanted because I was so done with guys dragging me along while they figured out their uncertainties. There is also nothing more attractive to me than a guy who is confident in who he is and where his life is at, and I just think it's hard to argue that you can say the same for someone who is thirty years old compared to someone who is thirty-five.

I came across this one guy on the app who shall be named German, and I thought he looked pretty handsome. He liked one of my photos on April 18, 2019, and I invited him to start the chat. He was 37 and I was 27 at the time, but that didn't raise any red flags for me. In our initial conversation, he revealed that he's a native New Yorker like myself, so our common background made our conversation easy going and natural. I also came to realize that meeting other native New Yorkers was rare, and it was cool that we could speak the same city language. We met at Attaboy, a speakeasy in the Lower East Side that offers fantastic cocktails, and the night went somewhat similar to the night I had with J. I didn't have any expectations for our date as usual, but we hit it off. I have a weird sense of sarcastic humor. If you get my type of humor, then you get it; but if you don't, then most likely I'll feel a little misunderstood and you'll think I'm weird. Thankfully, with German, he understood my humor and actually even added to it.

As we were conversing, I was throwing in some jabs here and there, and we were also ordering a lot of cocktails. I definitely had way more to drink than I should have. I don't know what it is, but every time I drink, I never want the night to end. I just want to prolong that euphoric feeling that alcohol gives me. I remember that I was so drunk that I was contemplating if we should go to another bar for another drink or if we should go grab some pizza. And we all know that there's nothing more satisfying than a slice of New York pizza, let alone a slice of New York pizza when you're drunk. He probably thought I was a complete mess, but he still stood by me as I was making the toughest decision for us for that evening.

Things got blurry here. I don't know what happened afterward, but I knew I couldn't drink anymore, and I wasn't really in the mood for food either. I also wasn't planning to go home with him, but I did. And looking back, I don't regret it because that's exactly what I wanted at the time, and I was acting based on my feelings. Sure, alcohol affected my decision, but I was single and was definitely trying to mingle.

I am also not afraid to check myself and say, yes, I'm aware that I'm a walking contradiction—as I had stated earlier that I was looking for something more serious at this point. But you ladies have to also remember that feelings change throughout the process of online dating, from the moment you decide to match with someone on the app to setting up the first date and meeting up with them in person. I also think there's a difference between my preference for someone's age versus my actions on a first date. I don't subscribe to any rules about dating, which I know sounds controversial, as I just stated in the first chapter that I would never say yes to meeting for dinner on the first date. But when I refer to these rules, I'm talking about these strict, concrete rules that you hear all the time. For example, the rule that you should never sleep with someone you just met on a first date, or that you should only have sex after you've been on X amount of dates with a guy, etc.

What works for one person will not necessarily work for someone else. And if you have these rules when you enter the dating scene, it limits your freedom and interferes with the natural flow of how things should go. Instead of following these rules, I follow my heart, and yes, I know that sounds cheesy, but it's true. I'm a big believer in being authentic to your feelings. I couldn't care less about what others think of me, even the guys that I meet on the app because, at the end of the day, this is my life, my experience, and my story. I'm going to do what makes me happy and what feels right at that moment.

I'm not exactly sure how my relationship with German developed afterward, but it was a special one because I felt like we had a strong connection that surpassed the sex on the first date storyline. Spoiler alert: German was the first guy from the dating app that I actually developed real feelings for, and he was the first guy that I saw exclusively for the next two and a half months.

He worked for a bank, and the combination of his position in his career along with his maturity and the overall way he carried himself was so appealing to me. Our dating phase occurred during the spring, so the weather was beautiful. We had a lot of dates—more than any person I'd dated thus far—that revolved around exploring NYC restaurants and bars, as we both loved to eat and drink. We had a consistent schedule in meeting up, and our usual dates would be a happy hour/dinner after his work hours with another weekend hang out to supplement the weekday date.

I loved spending time with German, and I think he equally loved spending time with me. I can say that we had a great balance of friendship and romance. He was a bit silly, and he brought that side out in me. The relationship was never that serious, and I think it worked perfectly with the spring season because the movement and progression was consistent and natural. As the weather got warmer, both of us wanted to always be out and about. I also just realized that we never had dates at his apartment like I have done previously with other men. We filled our quality time with NYC activities, which was a positive element in our relationship.

What I liked most about German was his company, his laid-back attitude, and his vibe. There was something so refreshing about his energy and one that I can only keep associating with the fact that he was thirty-seven. Also, he was six foot one, and he had these beautiful blue eyes that I could just stare into all day. I felt like he was a man, and all the guys I met before were boys.

I remember, however, about a month into our relationship, I felt a little bored and was questioning if we were progressing as a couple. That's also another issue with me because I'm the type of person that wants to be excited about life and doing something all the time. I'm also an Aquarius, which is an air sign, and that means I cannot be constrained to one place for too long.

I acknowledge that things can become routine after dating for quite some time, but I've always been the type to shake things up so I can still feel that excitement. I was going into our date, and I thought to myself, *This will be the date that I will determine if this will end or not.* Surprisingly, when I saw him that day, I felt the initial attraction and butterflies come back because damn, he looked good in that white button-down shirt.

That moment made me realize that a relationship can have its phases. I thought I wanted this relationship that was filled with constant action, but German made me realize that it's okay to simply slow down and just enjoy each other's company. We continued to see each other for another month or so, and it was great. The last date we had was at Chinese Tuxedo, a bar located in downtown New York City, and I loved the ambiance there. Nothing concerning happened on our date, but I think we both knew that our time was coming to an end without either one of us acknowledging or bringing it up.

I was moving to Brooklyn in a few weeks, and I remember thinking that the distance from my place to his Upper West Side apartment would be too much of a hassle. But in reality, I was using that as an excuse instead of being honest about what our relationship was at the time. In all honesty, our relationship had run its course. Again, we didn't have any arguments, and I can't say anything negative about the time I shared with German.

As I reflect on our time together, I can appreciate the security that he always gave me. German gave me reassurance, and that's one thing that I valued about our relationship. I read somewhere that if you have to question where you stand in a relationship or how a guy feels about you, that's a red flag. You should never feel confused about a guy's feelings.

The thing about relationships is that despite how things are at the surface and how good everything seems, sometimes, it's just not the right fit. Sometimes, you don't even need a reason or explanation to understand or accept that. The universe brought German into my life for a reason. I'm so appreciative of all the memories I've had with him, but it was also time for it to end because he was no longer serving me, and I don't think I was serving him either.

We didn't have an actual conversation about the relationship, but when we said goodbye that night, we both knew it was the final goodbye. My relationship with German was the last relationship I had as a Manhattan girl.

In some strange way, I think my move to Brooklyn was a new chapter for me, and I think German was the perfect ending to my dating stage as a Manhattan resident. If you're from New York, then you know that distance and boroughs play a role in your decisions when it comes to commuting. As a city girl, I never thought I'd move to Brooklyn, and when I was in the city, going to Brooklyn seemed like a mission. But in my heart and soul, I knew that saying goodbye to German was the right decision because I was making a fresh start, and I wanted to focus on my move and this new phase of my life rather than our ending relationship.

Dating is a process. I learned early on that it's actually more difficult to find someone or something that can go past the surface level and have all the stars align in terms of timing. However, I did find something special and unique with another certain individual shortly after, and his story is coming next.

KEY LESSONS

- YOU CAN SLEEP WITH SOMEONE ON THE FIRST DATE IF YOU WANT TO.
- SOME RELATIONSHIPS ARE MEANT TO LAST ONLY A FEW MONTHS, AND THAT'S OKAY.
- DATING IS A PROCESS, AND YOU HAVE TO TRUST THE PROCESS.
- A RELATIONSHIP HAS ITS PHASES.

THE ONE WHO GOT AWAY

AS I WAS GEARING UP for my move to Brooklyn, there were a few men who matched with me on the app. I'm not a pen pal type of dater, and I prefer to take things offline because I'd rather see if I have a connection with someone than give them too much information about me. I learned this the hard way because I did this in the very beginning stages of online dating. If a guy also doesn't ask me out, I have no problem being forward and presenting the offer myself as you are now aware of from my experience with J. I also put a lot of emphasis on energy because I believe this intangible concept holds more weight than communication through a screen. Sure, you can still feel energy virtually, but there's something about a physical exchange of energy with someone in person that speaks volumes for me. Energy, like "vibes," doesn't lie, and it further enhances your intuition and gut feeling. All of these are superpowers that we have, and for me personally, I like to tap into it by seeing how my energy mixes with someone else's.

I matched with this one guy named A. I recall thinking that he had an average profile, nothing that jumped out, but also nothing that was off-putting. He liked one of my photos on June 22, 2019, and I invited him to chat as I normally do when guys match with me. We had a few exchanges on the app, and he then asked if I was interested in grabbing drinks. He was one of the first guys on Hinge that shifted the conversation quickly from the app to meeting in person. Moving is a stressful time, and I could've easily said no, but I thought it would be a great opportunity to get my mind off of that dreadful and stressful process.

We met at The Winslow in the East Village on June 28, 2019, which fell on a Friday night. The doors were open as it was a beautiful summer day, and he was sitting in the chair closest to the edge of the right side of the bar. He instantly gave me good guy vibes. Like most women, I'm usually attracted to the bad guys, but there was something reassuring and invigorating about A. Our conversation flowed naturally. I could tell that he was an intelligent man, someone who values family and career, and had a great upbringing. This is always a good sign, because as I learned from therapy later on, someone's childhood plays a critical role in how they navigate relationships. The evening was going well, and we decided to grab food afterward. That's always a good indicator that things are moving in the right direction when the date transfers from happy hour to casual bites. I remember him asking me what I was doing that weekend, and I said nothing, except moving. He mentioned that he didn't have any plans and jokingly said that we could see each other again.

I was elated because I was having an amazing time with A, and since I didn't live by these dating rules, I figured *what the heck, sure*. I think that's also a testament to our connection. Some people might think that's too soon to be going on back-to-back dates with a guy I just met, but I trust my feelings and act according to them. It felt right, and that's exactly what we did.

He knew that I loved sushi (are you even surprised at this point?). He told me about an amazing place he could take me to that requires a reservation. He said he could pull some strings and get us in even though it was last minute. Whether or not he was lying, I didn't care because he won some major brownie points that day. This was something that I learned to appreciate about A. Even in the early phase of our relationship, he was always a gentleman who took the lead. A had a way of making me feel special and putting me first. He also planned a lot of our dates and took initiative, and I always admired that about him.

We met at a bar for a drink before dinner and then headed to this secret restaurant. In honor of our conversation, unfortunately, I can't disclose this place. But let me just tell you, the restaurant is as amazing as he made it out to be. I felt incredibly grateful to have experienced dining there with him. The restaurant had an atmosphere that took you out of New York City and into the heart of Japan. The food was amazing, the sake was delicious, and I was with A, so there was nothing that I would've changed about that evening.

It was surprising to know that we were only on our second date, because whenever I was with A, I felt comfortable and I felt safe. It's difficult to try and describe the exact feelings I had that evening, but I remember just looking at him and thinking, I was meant to meet him. He just had a positive radiance about him, and I also loved that he was driven. Whenever we spoke about personal goals, he always had this attitude about making his vision into a reality instead of just talking and dreaming about it.

Seeing each other and making plans was also very easy for us. The process of scheduling our dates was never a question or a struggle. Every time we would talk, he would mention what day of the week he was free; as long as I said I was free too, he would take initiative in choosing a place. It was that simple, and I wish most guys could take notes on his approach. We had another dinner date shortly afterward.

I remember our fourth date vividly, and only because this time, it was in Brooklyn. The fourth date was about two weeks after I moved, and we decided to do a day date on a Saturday. It was a scorching hot day, and we decided to meet at Brooklyn Bowl because we thought it would be fun to do an activity. I actually walked all the way there—a forty-minute walk in ninety-degree weather for reference—and it was probably not a smart idea because I was sweating. (This is also a perfect example of what makes me a true New Yorker. I love walking, and a forty-five minute walk is very normal for me. I know some of you think I'm crazy.)

When I arrived, thankfully there was AC, and I cooled down quickly. Unfortunately, there were no lanes available, so A and I decided to have a drink while we waited. After chatting for an hour, we realized that the wait was too long, and we no longer wanted to bowl. Instead, we decided to go to the William Vale, which is literally right next door.

We caught the sunset just in time, and it was a beautiful view. I still have a picture of us on this day, and I still remember exactly how I felt at that moment. As we overlooked Manhattan from the Brooklyn side, I remember telling him how grateful I am to call this place home and how much I love New York. He agreed, and he pointed to a random high rise and told me that he would live there one day. He quickly followed up his statement with something along the lines of, *It won't be too long. I just need a few more years.* And this is why I was falling for A. I never doubted his dreams and the fact that he was so sure about what he wanted for the future. The plans he made for his life were so appealing to me.

As it started to get dark, we planned to go back to my place, since I was only a twenty-minute Uber ride away. As I mentioned, I moved in only several weeks previous, but my building was one of those fancy new Brooklyn buildings that had a rooftop and all these cool amenities. Since we met at the time of my move, I thought it was appropriate to show him my place, finished or not. We hung out in my living room, and I remember that he looked into my eyes and told me that I was beautiful. I still remember his words sent chills up my spine because I knew his words were true and genuine. One thing led to another, and before I knew it, we were heading to my bedroom and things were about to go down.

Our sex life was great, but I think it's always a little awkward during the first time with a new person because it's hard to predict how the interaction will play out. Sex with a new person is unfamiliar territory in terms of knowing how their bodies move, what they like, etc. This time, unlike the previous encounters, I was completely sober, and I was in a mindset that wasn't affected by alcohol. At this point, I knew I liked A. After cuddling for a while, he ordered an Uber to go home. I actually appreciated his deciding not to spend the night. I know some women might disagree and prefer that the man stay the night, especially after you have sex for the first time with someone, but this was only our fourth date. I love my own space, so I was relieved that he didn't express the desire to spend the night with me.

This must have been close to a month of us dating, and I wasn't seeing anybody else at that time. I really liked A, if you can't already tell, and one thing that this relationship excelled at was consistency. A and I were consistent with talking during the week, with seeing each other at least twice a week, and we were consistent in our communication. I felt like he was my boyfriend, without the label, and there was no pressure in making us a thing. He was an individual who was whole and was in the process of building an amazing life for himself. He never gave me the feeling that he needed someone to complete him. The way he approached our relationship and the way he carried himself made me realize that he was open to love but wasn't desperately seeking for it. I felt like I was on the same wavelength, and I didn't try to fit myself in his world, either. I could tell something beautiful was forming, but instead of imagining us in a fantasy world, I was always present and enjoyed what we had.

I don't know how else to explain it, but this relationship was just working. We enjoyed each other's company and explored New York during the summer. In addition to the carefree spirit of the city along with having A's positive and laid-back energy, I was having one of the best summers ever. It was a lot of fun being exposed to all these new restaurants and bars. Although I've been a New Yorker my whole life, I felt like A opened up my eyes to what else the city had to offer. It's one thing to fall in love with the city, but it's another to do it with someone else.

Another reason why I knew I liked A so much was because time was never a factor for us. I know that I was concerned about this distance when I was with German, but I didn't care when it came to A. A lived in the Upper East Side, which is practically the same distance as German. I always wanted to spend as much time with A as possible. And one thing I want to mention is how caring and considerate he always was. Whenever we would end up at his place, I would take an Uber home late at night (or early in the morning, if you want to be technical since it was usually around 1–2 a.m.), and he always wanted me to share my ride status with him to make sure I got home safely. I'd like to point out that this isn't common for guys to do, as I learned afterward.

We continued to see each other, and we had reached the two-month mark as a couple. I remember I saw my friend Rochelle before going on a date with A and was just gushing over how much I adored this guy and how I saw a future with him. She was happy for me, and I was, too! My date with A went as it normally did. We always had a great time, and the date always ended well. I would leave with a big smile on my face, looking forward to the next time we would spend time together.

Toward the end of summer, A had a wedding to attend during Labor Day Weekend. It's wild to think that we met in July and saw each other consistently until September. I have to admit those two months were absolutely beautiful. A was everything I was looking for, and I was just over the moon that I met him. After the holiday weekend, we were texting, and I was waiting to hear back about his schedule so we could plan our next date. He texted me saying that he was still trying to figure out his work schedule, but there was something on his mind. Here is where we cue in the dramatic music.

He asked if he could call me, and I said yes. When we spoke, he mentioned that he was on an Uber ride going home. He began the conversation by telling me that he didn't feel like we were progressing in our relationship. His statement took me by surprise, and I was completely blindsided. I had no idea where this was coming from. I needed a moment to digest what he was telling me so I remained silent. He said, "I thought you felt the same way on our last date." And I told him that I didn't, and that I was so confused! I even asked him if I did something wrong. He assured me that I hadn't. I then challenged him and asked about the sudden change in his feelings. He then proceeded to tell me that he wasn't sure about what he wanted.

That response, ladies, is something that *I absolutely cannot stand.*

Now I have no hatred or anger toward A, but I just can't wrap my head around that statement because I thought A and I were on the same page since day one. I wasn't sure if he was having a fear of commitment or if this relationship was getting too real, but either way, I couldn't understand how he went from being into me and seeing me consistently for two months to wanting to end the relationship without any previous mentions of his feelings or doubts.

A was still such a sweetheart because, despite the unexpected news, he did ask if I was okay. I could tell from his voice that it wasn't an easy thing for him to tell me. He also said that if I wanted to talk later, I could reach out, and he was there. I'm not sure if he could tell how much that hurt me because it was really difficult for me to talk while I was tearing up. I composed myself and said, "Okay." Then we hung up.

I'm the type of person that feels all the feels, and when I feel, I feel instantly. Under my hard exterior, I'm sensitive and emotional, so all of this hit me all at once like a tornado. I'm not the type of person that takes time to process thoughts and emotions. I remember vividly that I was in my bed, and I just started crying like a big baby. The thing that hurt the most was the fact that I didn't see any of this coming. I had high hopes for our relationship, and what made it harder was the fact that he was such a good guy. I couldn't even hate him if I tried.

I went out to the living room because I really needed some support. I basically started bawling in front of my roommate and told her what happened. In a way, I was surprised by how emotional I got because I knew I liked A, but at that moment, I guess I didn't realize how much I did.

Looking back now, I think I should've reached out to A after our conversation to get more closure, because till this day, I still don't understand why our relationship ended. I can't say for certain that A made the right decision, but I can see where A was coming from. In my relationship with German, there was a point where I enjoyed his company, but I didn't feel like we were growing. Maybe that's how A felt about me and about us. There wasn't anything wrong with our relationship or our connection, but I think A wanted us to be consistently moving forward. And I think, in his mind, we had reached a plateau.

Out of all the men I've dated, A still holds a special place in my heart. I'm obviously over him now, but he taught me a lot about dating and love, and that's something I will remember forever. A lot of the men I've encountered afterward don't come close to A, and I have to admit that I would compare a lot of guys to him. He checked off everything I was looking for in a man, but even more so, he was considerate, thoughtful, and had a good heart. The vibes and energy he gave me on the first date are still the same vibes and energy he left me with. I've learned from our relationship that while looks and titles might be what we initially look for in a dating profile, it really comes down to connection and how a person makes you feel. When I think of A and when I recall our experience, I know I felt a glimpse of love. I'm not saying that I loved him, but I'm saying he gave me a feeling of what love could be. For that, I could never be upset with the way things unfolded.

I know that whoever ends up with A is a lucky girl. That girl isn't me, and I'm okay with that right now because everything happens for a reason. I know that the universe has a different plan for me. A came into my life for those two months to show me that love is possible and real and that there are good guys out in the world. He also taught me that I deserve to be treated like a queen. A showed me that I deserve love and that I should give love a chance.

As you can tell, A made a huge impact on me and played a critical role in my dating history. He could've been the one who got away, the one who broke my heart and the one who blindsided me. But through it all, I think A is the one who taught me the most I needed to know about love and dating, and I'm so grateful for that.

KEY LESSONS

- GETTING YOUR HEART BROKEN IN THE QUEST FOR LOVE IS INEVITABLE.
- THE WAY A MAN ENDS A RELATIONSHIP SAYS A LOT ABOUT HIS CHARACTER.
- JUST BECAUSE A RELATIONSHIP DOESN'T LAST DOESN'T MEAN THAT IT WASN'T SPECIAL.

8

THE ONE WHO TOOK MY INSTAGRAM PHOTOS

A GUY I'LL NICKNAME "AUSSIE" was the first man I met through Hinge who had an accent. His time frame is a bit difficult to pinpoint since I met him after I matched with A. But his story is interesting in the direction that our relationship took, so for timing references, just know that my interaction with him overlaps with my time with A.

As I mentioned before, I'm always skeptical to give out my social media profile to guys online. I never link my accounts to my profile. I don't even have my last name listed on Hinge because a quick Google search will provide all the information about me that I don't want guys to know, at least not right before getting to know me. I'm not saying this because I'm ashamed of what I do, but again, this stems from my desire to be somewhat private.

I matched with Aussie, and I have to admit that he was on the fence for me. I wasn't crazy attracted to his photos, but what intrigued me the most was his photography skills. I have a love for photography and travel, and I could see that those were things that he was passionate about as well. He was also from Australia, and whenever I come across a non-American on the app, my curiosity is immediately activated. I had never met an Australian guy before, and I go weak for accents, so I thought I'd give him a go.

After a few quick exchanges on the app, we decided to meet for happy hour a few days later. We met quite early at The Spaniard in the West Village for drinks. Interestingly enough, nobody was at the bar at the time, and I think the bartender could tell that Aussie and I were on our first date. I remember that the first twenty to thirty minutes of our interaction wasn't as natural as my first dates normally go. Aussie was clearly nervous and was more reserved than other guys I've met, but I was completely in my element. After he warmed up a bit and spoke about photography and his background, his guard was down, and we were able to converse without the awkwardness. I felt comfortable sharing what I did for a living and my Instagram with him because I knew that he spoke the same language, and we ended up bonding over our creative interests.

It was about 5 p.m. when we finished our drinks, and it was obviously still light outside. It was a beautiful summer day, so we decided to grab ice cream at Big Gay Ice Cream Shop, only a few blocks away. We enjoyed our treats at a park nearby like two young kids. This is the moment when Aussie leaned in for a kiss, and I gave in. It was a nice first kiss, and I didn't feel like he kissed me just for the sake of kissing me. His kiss felt passionate, and it ignited a spark in me. He then confessed that I was his first date from Hinge, which explains his nervousness in the beginning. When we were about to depart, he kept telling me how amazing I was. But I wasn't sure if that was because he hadn't been with someone in a while, or if he was just happy that his first date from an online app went well. Regardless, I did want to see him again.

My first date with Aussie happened during the beginning stages of me dating A. I think it's important to explore your options and not be tied down to one person, because from my experience, you never know how things will end up. Plus, your gut will tell you when you want to see one person exclusively. The second date I had with Aussie wasn't even really a date. We met at McCarren Park for a stroll one afternoon, and this is when we decided to explore Williamsburg and take photos. I had just bought a new Sony a7R III camera, and he offered to teach me the basics, going over all the features with me. He ended up taking some photos of me. They came out so great that they made it on the gram, so, yes, your girl was happy to kill two birds that day. I think we spent at most an hour and a half, and that was the end of our "date."

When I thought about Aussie, I realized that I just didn't have those romantic feelings for him, and I felt that our relationship was more platonic. I was into A, and I decided to see him exclusively. Aussie texted me, expressing his desire to see me. I wrote him a long message that wasn't entirely honest, but it wasn't exactly a lie, either. I basically told him that I wasn't looking for a relationship (the part I left out was that I meant a relationship with him). I also told him that I was busy with my move and that I wanted to get settled in and focus on that. He then responded with a longer message than the one I wrote, explaining that if I didn't want to be in a relationship that he was okay with that, but he wanted to see me again and was trying to persuade me to give him one more chance. He kept saying that he just wanted one more date, but this time, it would be just the two of us. He figured that having that alone time would help me make up my mind about him. I was conflicted, but I was also very flattered.

This man was pursuing me, and I didn't know what that felt like. I thought if he was willing to go out of his way to try and convince me to see him one more time, what did I have to lose by saying yes? I was appreciative of his efforts, and I liked that he was "fighting" for what he wanted. That's attractive to me because I'm not used to that. So I agreed, and he expressed that he wanted to cook for me and have a nice dinner at his place without distractions.

Learning from my experience with Brooklyn, I didn't want to put myself in an uncomfortable situation or feel stuck at his place. So we agreed on a night, but I told him that I had to meet a friend afterward. Yes, that was a lie, but I don't feel bad about it because I think it's fine to have an escape plan, especially if it's late at night, and you're at someone's place. And ladies, you already know this is a typical card in our playbook, and it is similar to having your girlfriend call you to make up a fake excuse about why you need to leave the date early.

Aussie lived in Fort Greene, which is a neighborhood that I've passed by, but haven't really explored or knew much about. It's actually such a cute area, and I could understand why he loved it so much. When I met Aussie at his place, he had just bought us some wine and had a huge grin on his face when he saw me. I could tell that he was looking forward to the evening, which made me feel happy because it was easy to absorb his excitement.

I'm embarrassed to say that I don't remember exactly what he cooked, but I think he cooked fish, which is funny since Brooklyn cooked me salmon on our last date. What is it about guys cooking fish for women on a date? I will say that I did enjoy the meal with the wine, and his place had a cozy Brooklyn vibe. He had plants scattered throughout the apartment, which gave it some personality and life. The layout of his apartment allowed for the natural light to hit perfectly toward the center of his living room, which created a spotlight effect on the couch. Surprisingly enough, we didn't watch a movie or show. Instead, we just talked, and I felt an intimate connection with him that I hadn't felt previously. It was a bit concerning because I was dating A. But then again, I thought, *Well, this is what the bachelorettes must feel, because I have two men competing for the final rose.*

After spending a few hours at Aussie's place, I left to go meet my "friend." I actually ended up going home, and I wasn't really sure how to feel because I was conflicted about where I stood with Aussie. Keep in mind that this was our third date, and this is the date that I felt would determine whether I wanted to see him again or not. It surprised me to know that I did want to see him again because I went into the date with zero expectations. Plus, I was already willing to kick him to the curb had he not been so persistent.

His actions afterward made the decision easy for me because when we tried to set up another date, he was flaky and his communication was poor. I could tell that our relationship was somewhat going downhill, but it didn't faze me because I was entering my second month of dating A, and he had my full attention.

I can't really explain how Aussie and I decided to remain friends without openly saying that we would have a platonic relationship. Communication between us didn't cut right away and he was there, but again, there were no romantic feelings between us. I think we both knew that we got along really well, so our relationship shifted to the friend zone. I'm not saying that I'm a psychic, but I also got the feeling that he was seeing someone, and he probably knew I was too.

Some might argue that I shouldn't have remained friends with Aussie while I was seeing A, but I don't think I had anything to hide. A didn't know about Aussie, and I didn't feel that he needed to know. But if it got brought up, I wouldn't have had a problem sharing the dynamic of the relationship. This part is where it gets a bit tricky because I might get judged for it. But as I've said over and over again, I live my life by my rules, and I do whatever feels right in the moment.

I'm not sure how this came about, but after Aussie and I determined that we were just friends, there were talks about going on a weekend getaway to explore more of the USA and to take photos. I am completely honest when I say that the main purpose of our trip was photography. He had access to his friend's car, so after doing some research, we decided to take a trip to Virginia. The total drive time was seven hours, so we decided to make it a two-day trip and stay overnight. I was a bit skeptical about the overnight part, but the way we planned it made me feel better knowing that we were getting a hotel to just sleep. We had to wake up early the next day to drive back since it was a long drive.

He picked me up early Saturday morning, and thus, our mini road trip began. Our first stop was in Philly. After that, we made our way to Baltimore and then finally stopped by Alexandria in Virginia. (Old Town Alexandria is such a charming place, and it absolutely stole my heart!) There were tons of photo opportunities along the way, and I have to admit that the photos that Aussie took of me are some of my favorite photos to this day.

We had dinner on Saturday night, but again, it was so platonic, and it didn't cross the line of feeling like a date. I was a bit drunk, but this is proof that there wasn't anything between us because nothing happened. Even when we got back to the hotel, Aussie didn't make any advances or move toward me. We simply slept, both at opposite ends of the bed, and there wasn't any cuddling, touching, or anything of that sort.

I was relieved that the night played out the way it did, because I did have some hesitations going in. When we woke up, we explored a little more of Old Town before driving back to the city. Overall, I enjoyed the trip and felt like Aussie and I were on the same wavelength. I didn't feel guilty about going with him because I considered Aussie a friend, and the way things went down during that weekend confirmed that for me.

During this time, I was seeing A exclusively, and Aussie and I didn't talk that much afterward. I think we planned to hang out and explore Brooklyn one day, but the plans fell through, and so did our communication and relationship. I don't want to assume anything, but I think Aussie had a lot going on in his life at this time, and since we were just friends, he didn't prioritize our relationship. I was totally fine with that outcome because I did get a sense that we were only going to be temporary friends.

As you can tell by now, my experience with Aussie was an interesting one because I'm not sure if many women would've been okay with the transition from an online date to a friend to a road trip buddy. I've heard from some of my friends that they have remained friends with someone they met on a dating app or have built professional relationships with matches, which I think is something we forget that is possible.

I've learned from my time with Aussie that while Hinge is an app designed for people to meet their person, at the end of the day, it's really just an app that connects two people. What you make from that connection and what you get out of it is up to you, and the outcome may be beyond your control. I never thought I would be able to meet someone that would be my companion on a mini road trip, let alone someone that would take my Instagram photos. But that's the fun part about dating and meeting new people!

As long as you are open-minded about the process of dating, I think it takes the pressure off of wanting to find someone right away because you just never know how relationships will evolve and how things will turn out. It's also interesting to see where my mind was at that time compared to where I am now. I'm currently not looking for someone to be friends with or to be my road trip companion. I'm actually interested in meeting men for the sole purpose of being one step closer to meeting my person. Just as you grow and evolve and enter different phases in your life—socially, emotionally, and mentally—so does your relationship and process with dating.

KEY LESSONS

- IT'S OKAY TO DATE MULTIPLE PEOPLE AT ONCE, AND IT'S OKAY FOR THEM TO NOT KNOW ABOUT EACH OTHER.
- YOU CAN HAVE RELATIONSHIPS WITH PEOPLE YOU MEET ON DATING APPS THAT AREN'T STRICTLY ROMANTIC.
- DATING APPS ARE JUST A TOOL TO CONNECT TWO PEOPLE WHO WOULDN'T HAVE MET OTHERWISE.

THE ONE WHO DIDN'T MAKE IT
THROUGH THE PANDEMIC

IN CASE YOU'VE BEEN living under a rock, we are currently in a global pandemic as I'm writing this. Just Google 2020 or COVID-19 if you have no idea what I'm referring to.

As summer was winding down, so was my capacity for dating. After things ended with A, I wasn't exactly in the mood to put myself out there again. On top of that, I had a busy last quarter of 2019, as I had tons of travel and work coming up. I also know that when it comes to dating, you need to not only be emotionally available, but you also need to be mentally and physically available as well. I never understood why people would go on the app knowing that they were going to be away for the next few months. I believe successful dating requires consistency and momentum, and those are two forces that are overshadowed by traveling.

Fast forward to early December, I found myself casually back on Hinge. I guess you can say I was giving into the cuffing season. I matched with this Canadian guy, and like Aussie, I was intrigued because I had never met a Canadian guy before. Also, I thought the stereotype that Canadians must be nice had to be true. I wasn't exactly sure what to make of him, but the beauty of dating is that you don't have to make any decisions right away. We had a few exchanges on the app, and he was trying to get to know me by asking questions. I completely understand that people have different approaches when it comes to dating, but from my experience, I prefer taking things offline. I knew I wasn't looking for a pen pal, so I didn't answer Canadian right away and left him on "read and unanswered."

I believe it was a week later when he messaged me on the app, saying, "Dear diary, where did the cute girl go." I thought that was a clever response, so I wrote back, *"Dear diary, I wonder when that guy is going to ask me out."* And ladies, that's how you initiate a date. He immediately followed up by asking when I was free and from there, we planned our first date.

I wasn't feeling my best that week, so I mentioned that I wasn't in the mood for drinks, but we could still meet up. Canadian mentioned a tea place in St. Marks, and I was down for that because I love tea. I arrived before he did and sat in the back to avoid the cold air from the entrance door. When I saw him enter, the first thing I noticed was his leather jacket, which I would soon learn is part of his signature look and wardrobe. I thought he looked somewhat badass and definitely wasn't what I expected.

I was really indecisive with my tea order, as I am with most of my food decisions, so I decided to try something that was featured on the menu. We ended up chatting for a bit and getting to know one another. He seemed like a nice guy. Unfortunately, I was not fond of the tea I chose at all and felt bad because I couldn't even fake drinking it. We were there for maybe thirty minutes and decided to go to a bar after. I had no intention of drinking, but the night was young and there wasn't anything else we could really do since it was cold outside.

We went to McSorley's Old Ale House located nearby and found a cozy corner to chat. I think he did a really good job with breaking the ice because he decided to play this game where we would take turns asking each other questions. I know you're thinking *that's not a game because the whole point of a first date is to ask each other questions.* But hear me out, our game was different. I felt like once he suggested this game idea, the pressure, seriousness, and awkwardness that is usually associated with first dates disappeared. This game also followed a quick speed dating round format. It was fun, and it gave me a glimpse into his playful side. The questions were random, and it was a good way to get to know both of our personalities and thinking styles.

I felt a sense of comfort when I was with Canadian. After a round of drinks, he leaned in for a kiss, and I went for it too. The night ended well, and I was open to seeing him again. We had a few more dates afterward. I went to his place one night to see his rooftop since he had a beautiful view of the Empire State Building. He lived in the heart of Times Square, so we often met around his area.

One of the best dates we had was spent at the holiday markets in Bryant Park. The holidays are one of my favorite times of the year, and it was such a magical experience to be able to enjoy the holiday cheer and energy with a guy that I was interested in getting to know more. My favorite part of that night was visiting the vendors and shops, watching people fall at the skating rink, and getting hot chocolate. Christmas was right around the corner, so there was a romantic feeling surrounding the city that night.

Canadian went to spend time with his family for the holidays, as did I. He was coming back to the city for New Year's Eve, and I had a dinner party to attend, but we said we would keep in touch for the night. My roommate and I went to this New Year's Eve party and had hopes that it would be a crazy evening. It didn't actually turn out to be that way at all. Instead, it was a classier event with great food but a much older crowd. We still had fun but knew that we didn't want that to be our last stop for the evening.

I was talking to Canadian throughout the night. He mentioned that I could stop by his friend's place afterward, but it wasn't a party, rather an intimate get-together. I thought that would be a little awkward since I was with my roommate and didn't want to put us in that environment. I also wasn't just going to leave her alone on New Year's Eve, since I had planned to spend the day with her, not him. Looking back, I think that also showed how I felt about Canadian. We were still in the early stages of seeing each other, so I wasn't head over heels. I'm sure if my feelings were stronger at that time, I would've definitely made more of an effort to meet him that night.

My roommate and I decided to go back to Brooklyn. Our good friend and neighbor was throwing a party, so we stopped there for a little before heading home. That night wasn't the best New Year's Eve, but it was decent and I couldn't complain.

Throughout January, Canadian and I continued to see each other, and he was the only person I was seeing at that time. He was a data scientist. I still don't know what that is, but I thought it was cool and suited his personality well. We had meaningful conversations, and I could tell that he was a hardworking individual who cared a lot about work and his future. If you have been piecing my dating experiences together, then you can see a common theme. I like guys who are driven, who are successful in their careers, and who I can have in-depth conversations with.

My birthday was coming up (and wow, I just realized I have now been on the app for a full year). I didn't have any plans since it fell on a Monday, so he mentioned that we could do a lunch date, which I was excited about. He said that it would be best to grab food at his building instead of anywhere outside because he worked near Times Square, and it would be too chaotic as we were meeting during peak lunch hours. I was okay with that. He worked for a very well-known news company, and I met him there in the afternoon.

I didn't know what to expect, but we basically ended up grabbing lunch at a cafeteria, which brought me back to my elementary school days. I built my own healthy salad, and we proceeded to a table on the second floor. It wasn't that I wanted more, but it was just not an ideal lunch. I'm not referring to the actual food, but I meant we couldn't really talk because there were people around, it was broad daylight, and he was technically still at work.

The whole experience was so awkward for me and I think I wouldn't have cared if it were any other day, but it was my birthday, and I was questioning why we were spending it the way we did. I think maybe an hour passed by, and he had to go back to work, and I left. I was pretty sassy and wasn't nice because I recall saying, *"Well, this was nice."* But I said it in that sarcastic, *I don't mean it*, tone. After I left, I checked myself and had to put everything into perspective.

It's the thought that counts, and I guess Canadian wanted to see me for my birthday. Even though it was only an hour at his job, that's still something. I texted him to apologize and to also thank him. That's another problem with having expectations and not voicing them. I had to learn throughout dating to either change those expectations or to be transparent about them because guys are not mind readers, even though I know the majority of us women often forget that.

I will admit that Canadian and I had a consistent relationship, but I think the timing really affected our progress since it was right in the middle of the holidays. I also think January is an odd month for a lot of people because everybody is trying to find their groove after the holidays, and the energy is not the same. That sentiment perfectly fits our relationship. I also felt conflicted about Canadian because I knew I liked him, but there was something missing and I kept searching for that "thing."

He was the main subject in a lot of my talks with my close girlfriends, and I just remember the common feeling I would mention was being unsure. The uncertainty wasn't whether or not we were compatible or where things could potentially go. It was more uncertainty on his end about his feelings. I should have taken this confusion as a sign, but I didn't because I was still holding onto hope that if I continue exploring things with Canadian, I would find the clarity I was looking for. Communication is everything, so I brought this up while I was with him. I would mention that I never really knew how he felt and that I thought he could do better in communicating. He even acknowledged that communication was an issue in one of his past relationships, so at least he was aware of it.

Just as I am the type of person to move at a slower pace with people that I see potential with, I had to respect Canadian's slower pace in opening up. I couldn't blame him for not being able to express himself clearly or vocalize his feelings because I knew that I had moments in my past with men where I wasn't comfortable or confident in speaking about my emotions. I just told myself to be patient because I never wanted to come off pushy or overbearing.

Like I did with Mr. Chef, I ended up inviting Canadian to one of my work events. I always consider this a step forward when I allow someone I'm dating to get a glimpse of my life outside of the relationship. Canadian was well aware of what I did and understood how much of a role social media played in my life. I was invited to the advanced screening of *Birds of Prey: Harley Quinn* in February. It was being held at a theatre right by his apartment on a Sunday evening. It made sense for me to invite him, and I was curious to know how the night would go, as he was now considered to be my first official plus one for this work-related event.

Before the movie, there were activities outside the theatre room, and the staff ended up giving us headbands with Harley Quinn's signature pigtails. I didn't think Canadian would be down to act silly with me, but he was the one who encouraged both of us to wear them and rock them throughout the whole movie. I still have the photos of us on my phone, which brings me back to that exact moment where we both embraced our inner child. I thought he was a great sport in not caring about his appearance and wearing a childlike pigtail headband. We ended up enjoying the movie and were also pleasantly surprised by having the cast show up!

Timing in a relationship is everything—as I have already reiterated in the previous chapters—and my relationship with Canadian was a constant battle with time. It often felt like time wasn't on our side, but for some reason, we were still trying and were both willing to see it through. After attending the *Harley Quinn* screening, we didn't see each other for the next two weeks because I was taking my mom to Barcelona for her birthday. Canadian also had a week-long ski trip with his family around the same time I was in Barcelona. We kept in touch here and there, so there wasn't complete silence. I saw him after I returned, and I felt like we were taking a few steps back in our relationship. Was I still interested in him? Yes. But were we moving forward? Not exactly.

To be fair, it wasn't either of our faults because we had so many interruptions in between including the holidays and our travels. The first time we met after our trips, we decided to go grab some tea at Alice's Tea Cup. I gave him so many kudos for doing that because I think it takes a real man to say yes to having tea on the Upper East Side. *(If any of you reading this are currently in a relationship, text your man now to ask if he would be down to have high tea with you, and let me know what he says.)*

We waited outside to be seated, and I remember looking into his green eyes, feeling like the butterflies in my stomach were waking up. There was definitely something between us, and I was willing to work through it. Our tea time and conversation were okay. I felt like we stayed on surface-level topics, and we were trying to pick up the pace from where we left off. Afterward, we decided to take a stroll through Central Park where we spoke a little bit about relationships, the complexities around them, and our perspectives on them, and I brought up the topic of communication again. I wanted to get clarity on where he stood. I didn't exactly get what I wanted out of him, and I think he could tell I was getting a bit frustrated.

We decided to go to a bar and grab a drink afterward since he had a dinner to attend that evening. After a few sips, I felt courageous enough to be honest. I simply asked him why he didn't tell me he missed me when he was away. I didn't know where the question came from and I know I sprung it on him out of nowhere, but I felt like that's what I was searching for. It was clear that I felt a bit empty because he wasn't expressive in his feelings about me or about us. I don't recall him ever complimenting me. And I'm the type of woman that not only wants reassurance, but I also need it.

He responded by saying that he sent me photos during his trip and that was his way of saying he missed me. Clearly, that's not the same in my eyes. I then told him exactly how I felt. I was honest that he's never made it clear to me how he felt about me, and I wasn't sure where our relationship was going. We had been seeing each other for close to three months, and we had reached more than ten dates at this point. I wasn't trying to have "the talk" with him because I wasn't sure if I wanted to be in a committed relationship. I just wanted him to be more expressive about his feelings. He then went on to say that if I was wondering if he likes me, the answer is yes. I felt better getting that out of him, but when I left that night, the void I was looking to fill was still there.

This brings us to March, and this is when talks of COVID-19 started to spread. There was so much uncertainty about the virus, but New York was still operating as usual. We had planned for a dinner date on March 13th, and I remember this date clearly because it was pretty much the last weekend before New York shut down. I also want to clarify that throughout all the men I've dated, including Canadian, I never spent the night at their place since moving to Brooklyn, and none of them stayed over at mine either.

I'm the type of person that loves my personal space (as I mentioned previously in A's chapter), and I love my nighttime routine. I'm one of those crazy girls who is loyal to her ten-step skincare routine, and I love sleeping in my own bed. I don't care what time of the day it is, I normally will still go home because I find comfort in my space. Tell me that at least one of you can relate and I'm not weird.

Since Canadian and I were planning to meet for an evening dinner, I didn't want to rush getting back home since it would be late. I also thought it was time for us to try and take our relationship to another level. So, I brought up the idea of staying over at his place for the evening, and he of course welcomed that idea with open arms. I was looking forward to the night because I thought that this would be the right move to see if our relationship could go any further.

We went to a random restaurant. We were the only ones there since this was when fear and anxiety started to spread throughout the city concerning the virus. After dinner, we grabbed a bottle of wine and went back to his place to watch *Love Island*. I remember when he brought the idea up, I thought it was stupid. (I have to disclose here that I ended up watching it months later, and I'm actually a huge fan of the show now!)

After watching a few episodes, we took things to the bedroom. I'll spare you the details, but you can imagine what went down next. It was pretty late at night and I was a little drunk, but after we had sex, we were both still awake. I really wanted to strip away his layers, so I started to ask him some serious questions about his childhood, family, and insecurities. I'm not sure if that was a good idea or not, but at that point, I didn't care. He opened up a little, but it was like pulling teeth.

I then asked him how he felt about our relationship and the pace that it was going. He said that it was definitely on the slower side, but he was okay with that. I agreed. I think the slow pace had to do with both the timing of the holidays and also the uncertainty that he was giving me. I mean, if I wasn't clear about how he felt, why would I feel comfortable in moving things along?

It was probably 2 a.m. or later at this point, and I was getting sleepy. He was going to shower afterward, and I ended up falling asleep. I'm a morning person, so regardless of how late I stay up, my body naturally wakes up around 7–8 a.m. When I woke up, he was already up and doing work on his computer (and for reference, this was a Saturday).

For some odd reason, I felt an energy shift in the morning, and I'm all about vibes as you are clearly aware of by this point. It was the first night that I was spending at his place, and I think many women can agree, but you would probably expect for the guy to still be in bed with you and maybe cuddle with you. None of that happened. He didn't even offer me coffee. As I'm writing this, a part of me feels guilty for feeling that, but come on, is that too much to ask for?

After talking for a little in the morning, I ended up getting ready and was planning to head out because I figured it would be best to get out of his way since I didn't really feel wanted there, anyway. When I walked out, the sun was shining and it was a beautiful day, so I decided to walk all the way from midtown to the Lower East Side to clear my head. Throughout my hour-long journey, I still felt this uncertainty about Canadian. Was it me wanting more than what he was giving me, or was it me trying to make something work that clearly wasn't meant to be? I thought spending the evening would be a great idea and would give me clarity, but I learned afterward that the night actually confirmed that Canadian is probably not my person.

That following week, New York went into lockdown, meaning everything was closed and everybody was instructed to stay home except for emergency visits. That was a scary time, and my anxiety went through the roof. Canadian texted me, asking how I was doing. I told him that the last few days had been really rough. He responded saying he'd been stuck in the apartment working from home, but he was going on walks in the evening. I just thought his response was ridiculous and a bit insensitive. His response made me feel like he didn't even read what I wrote. He didn't even ask more about how I was feeling after telling him I wasn't doing well. He made the conversation solely about him. With everything that was going on at the time, in addition to my anxiety, I felt like this relationship (if you could even call it that) wasn't worth saving.

I didn't respond, and that's why my relationship with Canadian is known as the one that couldn't and didn't survive the pandemic. If things were different, I think my relationship with Canadian could've been an interesting one because it occurred before and during a pandemic. There was a possibility that this could've made us stronger. If we could've survived it, I think we could've survived anything. But in all honesty, the reality is, pandemic or not, we wouldn't have survived, period.

My experience with Canadian taught me a lot about what I'm looking for in a relationship. I realized I am the type of girl who needs reassurance, verbal communication, and confirmation. Why is it so difficult for men to just flat out tell you how they feel? I've had my share of being in limbo with someone, and I just don't do well with uncertainty or that gray area. I understand that with dating, there's going to be an inevitable uncertainty phase because both parties are still trying to get to feel for each other, but there does come a point where clarity presents itself.

I knew throughout our relationship that I was missing something. I think I should've listened to my gut feeling from the beginning because ladies, that gut feeling is there for a reason and that gut feeling is always right. I don't ever want to change anybody, and my intention wasn't to change Canadian's personality. I did my part in bringing up what was bothering me, and the rest was up to him. He couldn't give me what I wanted in terms of clarity and reassurance, and there was no way for us to have worked out.

I've heard that love should be natural, that it should be effortless and easy. I'm not discrediting that love doesn't or wouldn't take work. I understand that it does. But I think it should be work that both parties are willing to make because both parties want the relationship to work. Since my last relationship, I haven't found that yet. At that point, I started to feel like love was becoming more rare. I wasn't giving up on the idea of love, but it was disheartening to know at that time, I had been on the app for more than a year and met tons of guys, but nothing was sticking. What made me feel better, however, was knowing that each time it didn't work with someone, I was one step closer to meeting my person.

I was also very aware of the situation of the world at the time. We were in a global pandemic for God's sake. I wanted to use the next month to prioritize self-care and my mental health. I couldn't be bothered with dating, and how on earth were we supposed to meet someone during this time? We were forbidden from leaving our homes. I wasn't comfortable even seeing my family and friends, let alone meeting a complete stranger from a dating app.

Dating while a pandemic was taking over the world wasn't possible, or so I thought . . .

KEY LESSONS
- TRUST YOUR GUT AND INTUITION.
- IF YOU'RE FEELING LIKE SOMETHING IS MISSING IN A RELATIONSHIP, THEN YOU'RE PROBABLY RIGHT.
- YOU CAN'T MAKE SOMEONE OPEN UP IF THEY'RE NOT READY TO.
- COMMUNICATION IS EVERYTHING.

10

THE ONE WHO I SCREWED OVER

THERE ARE ALWAYS EXCEPTIONS to the rule, and while I am reminding you ladies that when it comes to dating, it's the guys, it's not you, sometimes we have to be honest and say, you know what, this time, it's me.

It wouldn't be fair if I were to portray myself as an angel with no wrongdoings because, the fact of the matter is, I'm human, I have flaws, and I make mistakes. While I do believe that I have been true to my actions and have acted authentically and honestly in most of my dating history, there is one experience where I was not my best self. And this is the part where I will show you the ugly moments and shed light on my imperfect side.

A month into the pandemic, I started to realize that this virus scare wasn't going to end anytime soon. After managing my anxiety and changing my mindset to acceptance rather than fear, I started to crave human connection. I was alone, and I felt lonely. My roommate was home in Long Island, so all I had for company was me, myself, and I. I did have conversations and FaceTime sessions with my family and friends, but it just wasn't the same. As much as I love alone time, it's also human nature to crave human interaction, especially since I had literally been by myself for more than a month straight.

I found myself going back to Hinge, and I felt that it was time for a fresh start because this was during unprecedented times. I didn't really think it was possible to meet someone as I mentioned previously, but I was curious to see what was happening in the dating world. Plus, I was simply bored. I came across someone who matched with me whose job title said he was a registered nurse. Given what was happening in the world, I was intrigued because I had a newfound respect for people working on the front lines. His profile said he was five foot eight, and to be honest, I would've swiped left. We all have preferences, so please don't come for me for my honesty.

I didn't swipe left, however, and I was pondering on my decision for this nurse's profile for a while. He was attractive and had a photo showing his tattoos, and I think a guy with tattoos is sexy (not all, but most). I had zero expectations as usual, so I ended up matching with him. Just because you match with someone it doesn't mean you have to respond, so there wasn't any pressure in the beginning stages. The nurse and I spoke on the app, and I remember that our initial conversation revolved around the virus.

On April 21, at 4:46 p.m., he wrote, "Hello there :) how are you doing?" From there, our conversation started. I remember telling him how appreciative I was for what he was doing and asked if he was working with COVID-19 patients. He answered yes. He was very humble and said that he was just doing his job. Once I discovered that he was actually working on the front lines, I thought there's no way this could work out because I was still having a lot of anxiety about the virus and wasn't comfortable potentially meeting this guy in person.

His location on the app said he was from a town in Jersey, and though I'm not familiar with Jersey, I did know a friend who owned a restaurant in the town he listed. I mentioned the name, and he said he knew exactly where the restaurant was and goes there all the time. I couldn't believe it, so I texted my friend and asked if she knew him. She mentioned that she didn't know him personally, but that he had been a loyal customer of her family's restaurant. She also said that he went there with a different girl all the time.

I didn't know how to feel about that statement, so I mentioned that to him as a joke. He defended himself by complimenting the restaurant, and said the food is delicious and it's a good date spot. We continued to have good conversations on the app for a few days afterward before the nurse asked for my number. I gave it to him, and we would text here and there. I will say that he was very consistent with reaching out to me, and we were messaging during the end of April—about two months into lockdown by that point.

He asked if he could FaceTime me one day, and I thought, *Why not?* I had nothing better to do, so we had a FaceTime date.

It was the first FaceTime date I had, and it went pretty well, and there was a clear attraction between us. I discovered that not only was he a nurse, but he also used to be a DJ, so he showed me his music room and record collection at his home. I thought it was cool that he had a passion for music because, as you know, I love when people are passionate about things and it shows. He also revealed why he decided to become a nurse. I don't think it's my place to tell his story, but just know that his personal reason made me respect and admire him more than I already did.

I remember that he wanted to take me on a date, but I was still uncomfortable with that idea. Knowing that he worked at a hospital and was coming into contact with sick people didn't sit well with me, so I told him that I just wasn't ready for that. He understood, and we continued to have casual talks here and there.

As we were approaching the month of June, New York was handling the virus well and confirmed cases were declining. I couldn't believe that it was about three months into the pandemic, but I definitely was at a better headspace than I was in March. The nurse was still persistent about seeing me. I finally agreed to see him because he was removed from working with COVID-19 patients. He was transferred back to his original cardiology department since the virus cases were declining. He also mentioned that he was required to get tested regularly at his job and recently tested negative.

I know my decision to go on a date with him was a risky one, but I agreed to it because I was okay with the situation at the time. Things weren't completely back to normal in New York, but there was a slice of hope since outdoor dining was allowed in the city. We decided to meet in the Lower East Side for a drink. There were bars and restaurants that were offering take-away drinks, and we ended up getting two alcoholic drinks in these plastic bags that reminded me of Capri Suns, which I used to pack for lunch as a kid. I felt comfortable with the nurse, and our conversation was very natural. I didn't expect it to go bad considering we had already FaceTimed before, and we were comfortable in each other's company.

After our delicious drinks, we grabbed some tacos from Tacombi and enjoyed them picnic-style at Battery Park. Since he lived in Jersey, he had a car, which made our date easy in terms of commute. During the picnic, things went well, and we were bonding over our relationships with the hospital. I won't dive too deep into my past health history, but I had open-heart surgery when I was twenty-four because I needed to have a closure for my atrial septal defect. I was treated at the hospital that he worked at. So, when I found out that he actually worked in the cardiology department, I already felt this weird, instant connection with him. I think that's why I felt compelled to explore this relationship. My surgery experience in itself is a story for another book, but it has always lingered in the back of my mind whenever I go on dates.

I ended up telling the nurse all about it that afternoon. And unlike my conversations with previous men, I didn't need to explain myself or feel hesitant that he would judge me or see me differently. I could tell that he was still into me by the way he would look at me. And if anything, that conversation only brought us closer. I didn't need to explain the process or any technical medical terms, and he didn't really ask me questions either because as he was listening to me tell my story, he was also sending me comfort. Though he couldn't and wouldn't be able to fully empathize with what I went through, he had an insider's perspective as a nurse, and that was enough for me to feel understood. We kissed that afternoon, and I felt a burden lifted off my chest, as he was the first man that truly understood my trauma and how that significant moment changed the trajectory of my life.

When I went home, I realized that the nurse was a true, mature man. Oh, I forgot to mention that he was forty. I don't know why I forget to mention that detail, but I think it's an important one because he's the oldest guy I've ever dated. I think I also changed my limit from thirty-eight to forty during the pandemic because I was getting tired of my lack of matches and wanted to expand my horizon. The reason why I remembered to throw in his age was due to the way he carried himself. He was a mature gentleman from the first minute I met him to the last minute he dropped me off on our date. He would always open the door for me and always made sure that I was looked after. As you can assume by my awe for these basic actions, I wasn't used to them. His behavior was so unfamiliar to me that I started to put the nurse on a pedestal.

I was still talking to other guys on the app (nothing serious), but the nurse stood out from the rest because he was all about me. He made me feel like I was the only girl he was interested in. He would text me consistently, always telling me good morning and asking about my day. Our second date was an outdoor date because I love adventures. And when I say adventures, I mean any activity that frees me from my normal routine, whether that be something outdoors where I can get physical, exploring a new place or food, or saying yes to anything that I can add as a new experience in my life resume. I had also been stuck in my apartment for about three months, so I jumped on the opportunity to get outdoors. It was also nice that the nurse had a car because things to do in the city were limited without one.

We decided to visit a nature reserve upstate to do a mini hike. The drive was beautiful, and I felt this sense of freedom when I was in the car. I was embracing the wind in my hair as I had the windows down for the whole ride. It was like my first day out of prison. I was in such a good mood that I finally felt like my pre-COVID-19 self again.

When I'm in a good mood, I'm full of light and energy. I brought that to our hike, and the nurse and I had a great time exploring the reserve and surrounding ourselves with nature. Throughout our hour-long walk in the woods, we also had really in-depth conversations about life, relationships, and our visions and goals for the future.

We were aligned with our values, and I felt connected to him. It's always such a relieving feeling to have someone know your past and insecurities, accept you for them, and also share a similar positive mindset. I don't know how we brought up the age difference, but he asked how I felt about that because he was twelve years older than me. I explained that it didn't matter to me because

I prefer older guys, but that he was the oldest guy I'd dated. I was going with the flow, and I enjoyed the nurse's company. After our hike, we explored more of the towns surrounding the area. We ended up getting Greek food and eating it by the water. It was a lovely afternoon, and I left feeling like it was a great day date.

I'm the type of gal that analyzes everything. While I do live in the moment and go with the flow, I also like to decompress and reassess my life. After my two dates with the nurse, I would have these weekly conversations with two of my girlfriends to unpack my experiences and to walk them through what I was feeling and thinking. I remember that I had nothing but great things to say about the nurse. I always felt like he prioritized me and my feelings, and it was evident that he was feeling me. I never once doubted that he cared for me because he never gave me a reason to.

With that being said, his positive feelings toward me started to scare me a bit because I felt like he was way more into me than I was into him. Keep in mind, we had only been on two dates at this point, but I could tell that he was more than two steps ahead of me. I wasn't sure if I could catch up, let alone if I wanted to be in a serious relationship.

I don't know if I got too deep into my thoughts, but once I started to express these concerns to my girlfriends, I started to question my relationship with the nurse. There weren't any red flags, but it did concern me that things were moving fast emotionally on his part. My girlfriends told me that my feelings were valid and to just go on another date to see how that goes and if anything changes.

This process remains true to my mindset about third dates because, as I mentioned previously, this is usually the time that it takes for me to feel a guy out one last time before deciding if I want to see them again. On my third date with the nurse, we decided to meet in Jersey this time because he wanted to show me his neighborhood. I was fine with that considering I had never been to his town before, and I was open to exploring it with him.

Going into the date, I remember feeling hesitant due to all of my racing thoughts. I know that I wasn't my usual bubbly self, and I was a bit reserved. I was still trying to feel the situation out. We walked around and grabbed brunch at this restaurant that was opened for outdoor dining. It was the first time I dined at an outdoor restaurant, so the concept was foreign but gratifying for me. Afterward, we decided to grab some wine and fruit and head to the park. I was still on the quiet side because I was just confused about my feelings at this time. The nurse was still clearly very into me, and I just wasn't sure how I felt about that.

After the third date, I thought about everything and figured that I should get out of my head and go with whatever was happening with the nurse. One of my girlfriends, Selma, made a point and asked if I enjoyed his company. I said yes. She then asked if I usually had a good time with him, and I answered yes. Selma advised me since there weren't any real issues, I shouldn't look for them or make issues that didn't exist. I knew she was right, considering she's the sensible and logical one among my group of friends. She also reminded me that it was summertime and to just have fun. With that clarity, I continued to talk to the nurse.

We decided to go visit a winery on our fourth date because it was the first weekend that wineries were opening. On our drive there, I remember he brought up our last date and asked me about it because he could tell that something was wrong and my energy was off. I was completely honest with him and mentioned that while I do like him, I was scared that our relationship was moving too quickly. I told him that I felt like he was my boyfriend, and we weren't just dating. I also clarified that I wasn't sure if that's what I wanted, and I just wanted to have fun.

I know some of you might be thinking, *Well wait, Mariann, didn't you say you were looking for something serious?* Yes, you are right, I did say that. But that was pre-pandemic, and with it still going on, I figured it would be best to let things be since I literally had no idea what was going to happen in a week, a month, let alone a few months down the road. I just wanted to focus on my mental health and do things that spark joy. I wasn't focused on finding my person.

After I expressed how I felt, the nurse became understanding about my headspace. Even with his newfound understanding, he challenged me with the question: What's wrong with doing "boyfriend and girlfriend" activities? He stated that it was better for our relationship to be at its current stage, instead of making judgments and changing its natural course.

While I do think he had a point, I think it came down to the fact that we weren't on the same page. I'm not sure if it was because he was much older than me that he probably knew what we wanted and was acting like I was his girl, or if that's just his natural approach to dating. But I knew I wasn't on the same level that he was.

Our conversation didn't end on a bad note at all, and I was happy that I was able to communicate my feelings and he respected them. As we were getting closer to the winery, I was getting more excited because as you all know by now, I love wine!

When we arrived at the winery, I was in awe of how big the place was. There was probably one more party there besides us, but the tables were so spread out that social distancing wasn't an issue. We ended up going for the wine sample and a charcuterie board to share. The weather was beautiful, and I felt this sense of peace and happiness I hadn't felt in a long time. When I was enjoying my wine, I remember looking at the nurse and thinking he was such a wonderful guy. I was really happy to be enjoying that moment with him.

After the wine tasting, I felt a little tipsy. Tipsy is the stage where it's good to maintain, but also a teaser phase, where your rebellion hormones start to act up and you want to let it take over. We ended up getting a bottle of wine, and before I knew it, I was drunk. But this time, it wasn't a sloppy drunk. Rather, it was a *I love life* drunk (I know a majority of you know that feeling). I was floating on cloud nine, thinking I could conquer the world and nobody was going to stop me. Knowing we also had this huge winery all to ourselves added to my zest for life.

The nurse and I decided to explore the land before deciding to take our blankets out to lie down. I don't remember what the hell was going on with me at the moment, but I was horny and he was too. The next thing I know, my clothes were coming off, and our hands were all over each other. We were kissing, and it was getting hot and spicy. Before long, we were having sex right in the middle of the fields, with no one watching, judging, or stopping us. Yes, you read that right. We were having sex in public, in this huge piece of land, on the grass, in a winery upstate. I still can't believe that it happened as I'm writing this, but it did.

As I recall this wild experience, it's like a scene from a movie. Let's pause the screen for a minute so we can unpack what the fuck just happened. I want to bring some things to your attention just in case you missed what went down. Firstly, when you are having sex, you obviously want to be comfortable, right? The amount of comfort I felt at that moment is indescribable because I was one with nature, completely bare and naked (talk about feeling free!). Secondly, sex usually takes place in the comfort of your own home, or somewhere indoors, private, and quiet. This was not the case for us as we were on the lot of a damn winery, in the middle of bumblefuck upstate! The thought of anybody watching us didn't even cross my mind because aside from the fact that I completely blacked out, there were so many acres of land that I don't think we would've even been discovered. And thirdly, this was actually the first time the nurse and I were having sex. As a memorable first sex experience, I think this encounter ranks number one.

After we finished, *or should I say, he finished*, we put our clothes back on. While we were walking back to the winery, I thought, *What the fuck just happened?* I mean, I have no regrets, but it was the craziest, wildest experience ever. To say that I didn't enjoy it would be a flat-out lie. I'm still in disbelief that it even occurred. Looking back on it now, all I have to say is that was an experience I won't ever forget. I always tell myself, *Damn, that's one for the books,* and look at me now, writing about it *in this book.*

I've never thought about having sex in public, but if you have, then girl, yes, I totally get it now! And if you haven't but want to (not that you need anybody's permission or approval), just know that if you need a sense of encouragement or push, then this is it. You only get one chance at this gift called life, so don't hold back. Just remember, this is your story and nobody else's.

Since the nurse and I shared that unforgettable experience, it's no wonder why we continued to see each other. He knew that I loved adventures, and I was craving for a getaway. We decided that we should go on an adventure together (if any of you are taking notes, here's where you should write that I love adventures and hop on every opportunity when presented with one).

Neither the nurse nor I had been to Newport, Rhode Island, so we decided to look into that. He found a place to stay there, and I thought it was pretty nice. He ended up booking the room. I was shocked when he emailed the receipt because it totaled more than $1,000. I didn't expect the nurse to pay for our stay, and I wouldn't have had him do so. I had every intention of splitting the cost, but I also didn't want to drop $500 for a two-day getaway, not factoring in other expenses including gas, food, etc.

Let me first clarify that I love to travel and have no problem spending money on it since I have been doing it for the past several years. However, I am a rational spender and couldn't justify that price, especially since it was only for two nights. I brought up my concern, and we got into a little argument. He claimed that when he sent me the place for approval, he thought I said yes, knowing the nightly rate. I argued that I wasn't aware of the rates, as I was only judging from the hotel's photos and reviews. We then agreed that it would be best to cancel since he was on my side that the pricing was a little extreme for a weekend getaway.

He couldn't get a hold of the hotel at the time since it was late at night, but he texted me early in the morning saying that the hotel called him back and allowed him to cancel for free if that's what I wanted. I said yes because when I was looking for restaurant reservations for the weekend, nothing was available anyways. I thought if we were both going to explore Newport for the first time, I wanted to do it right and do it well. I was confident that we would be able to find an alternative plan, so we decided to cancel.

We settled for somewhere upstate since Newport and Cape Cod—the two places we were interested in the most—were popular weekend destinations for the summer. I stumbled across Saratoga Springs and figured that would be a cool place to spend the weekend. After researching different hotels, we decided on one that looked nice. He was at work at the time, so I decided to book it under my credit card, and the total came out to be a little over $600, which was a more reasonable price, coming out to be about $300 a night.

I believe I booked the place on a Tuesday, and we were leaving that Friday. That week, I was experiencing anxiety, and that's something that I deal with every now and then. My anxiety didn't have anything to do with the trip, but rather, it was personal. I was also getting my period that week so my mood was off. I shrugged it off and didn't pay any mind to it because I figured a getaway might do the trick in shifting my mood to a more positive one. The nurse also had a hell of a week at work, so we both really needed the mini-vacation, and we were looking forward to the weekend together.

On the morning of that Friday, I still wasn't feeling my best and had somewhat of a stomachache, but I pushed through it. I told him in the beginning when he picked me up just so he was aware of what I was feeling. We stopped by a cafe to get some juices, and we were on our way to Saratoga Springs. I don't know what it was with me during the drive, but my doubts started to creep up on me again, and I didn't feel as crazy about the nurse as I did when I was drunk. I thought that maybe it was a combination of my lack of sleep, my indigestion, and my anxiety, so I decided to just shrug it off and be present. When we arrived at the hotel, we got settled before we decided to explore the town as we had an hour or so to kill before dinner.

I still wasn't feeling my best, but I was trying to put on a positive face. Throughout the dinner, I don't know what it was, but I was completely out of it, and I simply wasn't having a good time. I started to see the reality of everything and realized that I was using the getaway idea to satisfy the explorer within me. I was saying yes to the thought of going away because I selfishly wanted to travel, to get out of the city, and to have a change of scenery. But when I started to strip that layer away and looked at the reality of the situation, which was me going away with this guy, I wasn't completely into that idea.

Once that realization presented itself to me, I completely took myself out of my own body and was not present. I started to fall into my moody self, and I felt myself giving into this funk and place that I knew wouldn't be a good idea. As I've mentioned before, I'm all about vibes. I know energy is contagious, so I could tell that the nurse was absorbing all of this negativity from me. I wanted to snap out of the mood I was in, but I literally couldn't.

I know some of you are wondering, why not? Why can't you just make the most of it considering you're away with this guy? If you don't know my history and struggle with anxiety and mood swings, then there's no way for you to truly understand the state that I was in. After dinner, it was still early, so we decided to go to a wine bar. I felt really bad for the nurse to deal with my unpleasant mood that evening, but I'm telling you, it's like something took over, and I couldn't change my energy.

The moment where I realized it was a real issue was when he made a comment that brought me back to a version of my past self that I'm not proud of. He said, "I can't even talk to you right now because I feel like I have to walk on eggshells." I remembered my ex-boyfriend said something similar to that effect, and my mood swings were an ongoing issue for us. His comments didn't make me feel good at all, and I started to feel completely bad about myself and felt like something was mentally wrong with me.

I know I wasn't enjoyable to be around that night, but the

nurse still put up with me. We went back to the hotel, and I couldn't sleep at all. I ended up going down a Google hole by searching mood swings and issues. I concluded that I needed to get this looked at because I knew something wasn't completely normal about the way I acted or what I was feeling.

The next morning, we had an open conversation, and I apologized and told him that I believe something was seriously wrong with me. I told him that it wasn't the first time that I'd had one of those moments, but it had been a really long time since I'd experienced that type of episode. We decided to move past that night and just enjoy ourselves since we had one more full day at Saratoga Springs.

I ended up getting my period that morning and didn't have any pads or tampons with me. I was also experiencing bad cramps, so the nurse, being the gentleman that he always has been, decided to go to Walgreens and buy me tampons. This is something you see in movies and read about in books, but I never thought someone would actually do this for me. He kept the photo of the tampons I told him to get when he was there, and I confirmed it was the right one.

When he came back with my tampons, I thought this was probably one of the nicest things a guy has ever done for me. After I got myself ready for the day, we decided to simply walk outdoors, get some breakfast, and visit the shops. The weather was shitty since it was raining on and off, but we still tried to make the best of it. As the day went on, my mood was better, but the feeling that I had toward the nurse remained the same.

I realized at that moment that I just wasn't into him.

I also remember wanting to go home that day because Saratoga is actually much smaller than I thought. There also wasn't a lot of options for fun activities, and there were only small shops around. Since it was only a two-hour drive from the city, I remember thinking, we could just drive back this afternoon and not spend another night. I didn't even care that I would lose the three-hundred dollars. This just goes to show how I was feeling at the time. I obviously didn't bring this up, and I decided to just suck it up because I was going to be home tomorrow.

The rest of the day went fine. I tried my best to not bring any bad energy, but I also wasn't my typical happy, energetic self. I was just there, moving along and waiting for time to pass. Fast forward to the next morning, we were getting ready to go back home, and I was relieved. It's pretty sad to be this honest about the situation because I know it wasn't what he and I wanted, but I'll talk more about what I took away from this experience later.

When he dropped me off at my place, I knew that he didn't have a good time with me. We kissed goodbye, but the way we left off was different from how we usually leave off. And I obviously didn't like it, but I couldn't change it and couldn't help how I felt.

I didn't sleep much at all that weekend because I was deep in my thoughts and my anxiety was running high, so I ended up taking a much-needed nap that afternoon. I woke up with a new sense of clarity. As I analyzed the weekend, I felt completely horrible about the way I acted. I couldn't justify my actions and felt beyond embarrassed by the way I carried myself. I couldn't help it, but I felt worthless. I texted the nurse apologizing for my actions and thanked him for putting up with it. He responded later in the evening saying that shit happens, and it's okay.

I knew that was the end of our relationship. The next week was one of the worst weeks I had in 2020 because I found out about a friend's passing the following Friday. I was a complete mess and was emotionally shattered. It was the Fourth of July weekend, and I was spending it in Long Island with my roommate, so it was the perfect time to get away and not be alone in my apartment.

That day and the day after were extremely rough for me. I was processing the news, and I was grieving. On top of that, I was already feeling like complete shit about what happened the week prior with the nurse.

On that Sunday, my roommate and I were lounging in the sun and enjoying some afternoon sandwiches and snacks that her mom made. I was hanging out and trying to relax when I received an unexpected long message from the nurse. He basically told me that he wasn't going to write anything to me but wanted to explain how he felt after our weekend together.

He mentioned that at the beginning of our trip, when he was getting us coffee and coming back to the car, he saw me on the Hinge app. He admitted that it was not a good feeling to see me on the app considering we were about to spend the weekend together. He said it made him feel like a complete fool. He had contemplated whether or not to say something or if he should just make the best of it since we were already on our way. He then continued his long message explaining that it was a shame about how things went down because he really liked me. He ended his message saying that I didn't need to respond, but he wanted to let me know how he felt because it had been brewing in his mind for a week.

I was stunned by what I was reading because, if I'm going to be completely honest with you all, I don't remember being on the app when I was waiting for him to grab us some coffee. I replied honestly that I didn't remember opening the app or engaging with anybody on it. I sincerely apologized, but I wasn't going to make up any excuses. I owned up to my actions, and I told him that it was immature and inconsiderate of me to even do that. I told him that he was such a great guy and that he deserves someone who can match his character. I told him that I was sorry that he had to put up with me and my mood swings and that it wasn't fair for him to have the weekend that he did because of the funk I was in. I told him that he deserved better and that I was extremely sorry that he had to experience the worst version of me.

I meant every word I wrote to him, and I have to live with myself by going over and over in my head how unpleasant I was that weekend and knowing that I have painted myself in a negative light whenever he remembers our last encounter.

Now that I got everything out in the open, I want to first explain where I was coming from with all of this. In my defense, I was probably looking at the Hinge app as almost a natural thing like checking your email or Instagram. While I was waiting for him in the car, I was simply just looking at my phone as I normally do. I wasn't talking to anybody on the app. Does that make it right?

No. Should I have done that? No. Was it disrespectful? Absolutely, yes. I understand that I was in the wrong for doing that. If it was the other way around, I probably would've lost my shit too.

In knowing what the nurse knew going into our weekend getaway, I can't help but commend him for his character. He's a gentleman, without a doubt, and the fact that he remained a gentleman even after the crap I put him through says a lot about who he is as a man. Afterward, I did consider that I should reach out to him because I wanted to make it right, but I thought it wouldn't help the situation.

My experience with the nurse taught me that there are things that I still need to work on. If I'm going to be honest with myself, looking back now, I think I took advantage of the nurse's feelings for me, and that's not something I am proud of. But being able to acknowledge that has allowed me to become a better person. During 2017, the year that I took off to find myself, I thought my self-work was done. I thought I had completely found myself, and I was in a good headspace. I'm not undervaluing that time or my progress, but I've learned that just because you've done some self-work at one time in your life doesn't mean you are done forever. I took that experience to heart because it wasn't my finest moment. I'm not proud of the way I acted or the way I handled that situation. That experience was a wake-up call to check myself and to improve on that area of myself because I don't like the person I was during that weekend. I don't want anybody to experience that version of me, ever.

I'm proud to say that shortly after, I decided to start seeing a therapist for the first time in my life. I spoke about that experience with the nurse to my therapist, and we unpacked the situation, my mood, and my triggers. I'm currently working on finding solutions and methods to handle my mood swings and random outbursts. I don't think the nurse realized that he gave me a gift, and that gift led me to have an honest conversation with myself. My experience with the nurse was no longer about dating. Instead of focusing on whether or not I had feelings for him and how compatible we were together, I started to realize that my priorities should be focused internally. He was my mirror in a way, presenting me with a reality check of the areas that I needed to work on to better myself.

I also realized that I'm not really ready for dating. If I can't fix my personal problems, there's no way I can enter into a relationship because it will for sure be a formula for disaster. While I would love to preach about *we as women are never in the wrong*, I can maturely acknowledge that in this case, I was completely in the wrong. I fucked up, and I fucked up badly. Instead of playing the victim and having a pity party, I've learned to grow from this experience to become a better person.

I'm not happy at all about how things went down with the nurse. How our relationship ended is definitely one of my biggest regrets/lessons from my dating experience, but I'm also grateful to have gone through this turbulent time in my life. The experience taught me a lot about myself, and it gave me a new door into therapy that I probably wouldn't have entered had it not been for the nurse. Another thing I realized is that if something doesn't feel right, you should acknowledge it. Like my experience with Canadian, I had a gut feeling that something was missing. I also think that if I need to question a relationship, then that should be enough to tell me that it isn't exactly what I wanted.

Throughout the month I spent with the nurse, I kept going back-and-forth. I was trying to figure out how I felt, and I guess it didn't help that this was during a pandemic because that definitely affected the situation. I also felt a sense of obligation to see more of him due to the fact that he understood my health condition. Looking back at everything now, I can see that I couldn't separate my feelings about him and our relationship from my feelings about what the relationship was giving me, including freedom and a sense of escape. The activities we did were fun, but they clouded my judgment about him as an individual. I'm not trying to justify my actions, but I'm also acknowledging why I went about the situation as I did in that moment.

I believe in karma because what goes around, comes around. While the nurse goes down as the guy I screwed over, I had someone screw me over shortly after, and I guess I deserved it.

KEY LESSONS
- WHEN IT COMES TO DATING AND RELATIONSHIPS, ASK YOURSELF IF YOU LIKE THE GUY OR THE IDEA OF THE GUY.
- DON'T LET ANY COMMON GROUND YOU MAY SHARE WITH SOMEONE TAKE PRECEDENCE OVER THE CONNECTION.

- IF YOU HAVE UNRESOLVED ISSUES WITH YOURSELF, IT'S DIFFICULT TO NOT LET THAT BLEED INTO YOUR RELATIONSHIPS.
- BE INTENTIONAL WHEN IT COMES TO YOUR DATING LIFE.
- WHEN YOU MESS UP, TAKE RESPONSIBILITY AND ACCOUNTABILITY FOR YOUR ACTIONS.

THE ONE WHO SCREWED ME OVER

I TOOK THE ENTIRE MONTH of July off from dating and spent the month grieving over my friend's passing. July was a rough month for me to say the least, and I also spent the month going to therapy. I found it helpful to discuss my issues with someone I didn't know who was also licensed in the field. I felt a sense of improvement at the end of the month and was in a good place mentally and emotionally, so I decided to stop therapy, temporarily.

In August, I decided to redownload Hinge. The app was completely removed from my phone for the entire month of July because I couldn't find the time or a reason to incorporate it into my life. The thing about online dating is that the choice to go on the app coincides with how you're feeling in your life at that time. I wanted to take a peek, and that's what I did. I matched with this French guy, and he seemed to look great on paper. He was six foot two, thirty-two years old, and he worked for a technology company. He was attractive, and I was intrigued because his profile said he was from France. He had a business degree and earned his master's at Columbia University. He seemed well traveled and also loved adventures, so I knew we would bond over our shared interests.

We matched on July 21, 2020, and he complimented me by commenting on one of my photos. He said, "Beautiful picture :)." We had a few exchanges on the app and covered the basics, like where we were from and what we were up to. We quickly exchanged numbers. When we texted, we both realized we had flexible schedules and decided that our initial first date could be a casual afternoon stroll in the park. He lived in the East Village, and I mentioned that I was a huge fan of Tompkins Square Bagels. I was craving The Weezer (one of their specials), so he was down to meet there on a random Wednesday afternoon. When we first met, I was taken aback by his accent because I almost forgot that he was from France. I have a thing for accents, so I was looking forward to getting to know him.

After we ordered our bagels, we went to a nearby park. We had an amazing two-hour conversation about everything—including our love of travel, our upbringing and family dynamics, our values in life, and what we're looking for in a relationship. Everything seemed to align, and it was very strange how like-minded we were.

Since he grew up in France, he traveled a lot, and it impressed me knowing that he spoke four languages including French,

German, English, and Mandarin. I could tell that he was a jack of all trades, and I was fascinated by him. He made it clear that he was looking for someone that he could see himself with in the future because a lot of his friends were settled down, and he eventually wanted that too. I felt better knowing that we were looking for the same things, at least down the road.

After our serious conversation, I think we ended up kissing, and this is when shit took a turn. There was an undeniable chemistry between us, and I enjoyed kissing him. He proceeded with being extremely honest about how he was feeling at that moment, telling me how attracted he was toward me and how I was turning him on.

I was so confused because I wasn't even doing anything! I was literally sitting right next to him on the bench, minding my own business, being present, and just casually talking with him. I was, however, flattered because, I mean, who wouldn't be if a guy is telling you how much you are turning him on (without trying might I add).

I told him that it must be due to COVID-19 because there was sexual energy from everybody in the city but he was convinced I was the source of his arousal, and not the pandemic. He assured me that he was naturally attracted to me. He was very vocal about what he was feeling and saying all the things he would do to me. I was a bit thrown off guard and didn't know what to make of it. Was he just horny and just wanted to meet someone that he could fuck? Was this a cultural thing because he was French and French guys have a different approach to dating? Regardless, I knew I needed to assess this situation when I went home.

I think if he was an American, what he did and said would've been a total turnoff. But I guess because he was French, and we spoke a lot about his upbringing, I gave him a pass. I wanted to dive deeper into the situation. I spoke with some international friends, and they told me that that's just the French way of approaching dating. Apparently, French guys know what they want, and they go after it. And unlike in America, in France, there isn't this gray area of dating or pressure for labels. If they like you, then you know it, and basically, you go from zero to one hundred. (If any of you are in a relationship with a French man or have dated a French guy, please let me know if this behavior sounds familiar. I am very curious to explore the cultural differences in other countries when it comes to dating.)

With that realization, I decided to give this French guy another go. We ended up having two more lunch dates, and both dates went well. He always made it clear how attracted he was to me by the way he would kiss me or look at me. But what I liked best was that we consistently had in-depth conversations, and I felt like I always learned something valuable from them. Reflecting back, it was our conversations that kept me around because if they didn't have any substance, I wouldn't have continued speaking with the French guy. I'm not the type to have compliments solely win me over.

Within the third week of us talking with each other, he had planned to go to Cape Cod for a week. He wanted to see me the night before he left, but I already had plans. He was persistent and said that he could come to Brooklyn if it would be easier for me. I was able to see him after all, since my plans ended earlier than expected, and I thought we could grab a quick drink at a nearby bar where I lived. He agreed, so when we met up, again, there was this apparent sexual tension and energy between us.

I knew nothing would happen because I wasn't going to take him back to my place, and I wasn't going back to his place in the Lower East Side. After all, I lived only five minutes from the bar, and you already know how I feel about spending the night at a guy's place. He mentioned that he really wanted to have sex with me. I just laughed and thought, *That's great, but that's not possible or going to happen.*

To be honest, when he brought it up, I wanted to have sex with him, too. He knew that he was going away for a week, and he said that he really needed to have that time with me before he left. I still didn't think that was in the cards, and I told him that we would see each other afterward. He then sprung the idea of getting a hotel, and I thought it was a ridiculous idea! He was leaving tomorrow early in the morning, and again, the thought of being so close to home was a convenient plan for me.

We got into a little argument, and I kept coming up with reasons on why we couldn't and shouldn't get a hotel. He argued by saying that he's a problem solver. The issue was that we both didn't want to use our apartments since we had roommates, so he presented me with a solution. He went on to say how crazy he was about me. After he made his case, I thought, *You know what.*

It's a Saturday night, I do like this guy, and I actually wouldn't mind having sex with him. I'm all about going with the flow, so why not?

I agreed to spend the night with him, and he ended up booking a room at the Marriott Downtown near Battery Park. The next thing I know, we were in an Uber going to a hotel to have sex. (I know some of you might be rolling your eyes and thinking, *Damn, this girl never learns, and she's such a hypocrite.* But please bear with me. Let me share these memories without any judgments, please.)

Once we got the key to our room, it was strictly business. We had sex, and as expected, he fell asleep shortly after. I could tell he was in a deep sleep because he was snoring. When people fucking snore, they are obviously not aware of it, and I simply can't stand the noise. It was around 1 a.m., and I tried to go to sleep myself. I checked my phone shortly after to see that it was now 1:30 a.m., and then I checked again at 2 a.m. And both times, this motherfucker was snoring, and now more loudly. I was getting a bit frustrated because I really wanted to sleep, and I have a special relationship with sleep that comes first before any man.

I desperately tried to ease my mind and calm my thoughts, but it was a failed attempt. I looked at my phone after a while to see it was now 2:30 a.m. The thought of being in my own bed was so appealing that I checked how long it would take me to get home. The journey would only take twenty minutes. I kept going back-and-forth in my head, wondering if I should just stick it out and try to sleep or if I should leave. I didn't owe anything to the French guy to spend the night. I got what I wanted from it, so I decided to just get the fuck out.

I gave a little tap on his shoulder and nudged him. I said, "Heyyyyy . . . so I can't sleep. I think I'm going to head out." He was half awake and mumbled, "Why?" I mentioned that I was just having anxiety and wanted to be in my own bed. He asked what time it was, and I said close to 3 a.m. He thought maybe it would be best for him to go home, too. I told him to just sleep because he didn't live that far from the hotel and he could get in a few more hours of rest. He said, "Okay." After that, I put on my clothes. Then I grabbed my jewelry, my bag, and my phone and decided to peace the fuck out.

I called an Uber on the way to the elevator and went downstairs. There was a guy standing outside. He asked me if I was waiting for an Uber, and I responded, "Yes." He asked where I was going, and I said home. He laughed and said, "Oh, I thought this was home," as he pointed to the hotel. The situation was actually pretty funny because people stay in hotels for the night as visitors, but there's little me in the corner waiting for an Uber to actually leave the hotel to go home. He then said, "Oh, so you were meeting your man?" And I laughed and said, "Ehh . . . something like that." And he laughed too and wished me a good night.

My Uber arrived right then, and I was so happy to be going home. I arrived a little after 3 a.m., and I quickly took off all my makeup, brushed my teeth, and went to bed. That feeling was pure bliss.

The French guy texted me in the morning. He told me how lovely it was to spend the evening with me and that he was on his way to Cape Cod. I told him that I enjoyed it too, and we talked a little that day. I'm not a huge texter, especially when I knew he was going on a trip. And I actually was also doing a mini getaway myself in a few days, so we didn't talk for a few days after that.

On Friday, I was upstate, and I decided to give him a quick text to ask how Cape Cod was. He told me it was nice, but he was actually slammed with work and was stressed. I sent positive vibes his way, and that was that.

I remembered that he was coming back either that following Sunday or Monday, so I texted him Monday evening to ask if he was back. He said yes. We both did a little recap about our trips, but I felt like something wasn't completely right in the way he was texting. His responses and the quality of his communication felt a little distant, so I asked if he wanted to meet up later in the week.

He responded, "Maybe. I'm actually very stressed with work right now so dating isn't a priority. It's a bit too heavy in my head and heart."

What the actual fuck!

I thought his response was the lamest excuse in the world, and I didn't respond.

I wanted to give him the benefit of the doubt because, to be honest, I can't say for sure what he was going through. And I can't be too judgmental about his response. I just know in my gut that it was somewhat bullshit because his mentality and approach were completely different from the week prior.

Before he left, he was telling me how much he liked me and

how much he loved spending time with me. Now he was saying that he didn't want anything to do with me? I didn't give too much effort into unpacking it because I honestly couldn't give two shits. Did I like spending time with the guy? Yes, you can say so. Did I want to get to know him more? Yes, I wouldn't mind. But did I see a future with him and *like* him, *like him*? Not exactly.

I couldn't help but think that maybe he used me for sex, and once we fucked, he was done with me. I am almost certain that he saw me as "easy" and immediately put me in the non-relationship category that night. The only reason why I didn't allow that thought to affect my self-esteem and dignity was the fact that as much as he wanted to have sex that night, I did, too. I didn't say yes to that evening because I felt forced, manipulated, or pressured into having sex. *I said yes because I wanted some dick.*

I think sometimes guys forget that girls have needs, too. While they might feel proud that "they got it in," we ladies can say the same. There's such a double standard when it comes to sex for men and women, and I'm here to shed light on that. I knew when we were heading to the hotel in the Uber that we would have sex because I was giving him permission. At the end of the night, I knew I had the power but I wasn't trying to hold that power or do any of that shady shit. I got what I wanted that night and so did he.

I contemplated whether or not to include him and my experience in this book because the way it ended with him rubbed me the wrong way. I also wasn't sure if I wanted to share this experience with the world because I was a bit shameful in saying yes to getting a hotel for the night. But the current, more mature version of me today is offering self compassion to the version of me at that specific time. But I also want to be honest about the variety of men that I've met. I also want to show that I'm not perfect in selecting men, as there's no way of knowing someone's true motives. Whether the French guy intended to just have sex with me or not, I am okay with that now due to my own intentions and goals for the evening. I told you all that I believe in karma, and maybe I saw this coming after my experience with the nurse. Regardless, I've accepted how things ended with this French guy because he clearly wasn't my person.

Just remember, ladies, that when it comes to dating, you have to stand your ground. The reason why I left this situation without a bruised ego is that I made the decision for me, and not for him. Always be comfortable and confident in your decisions. That way, no matter how things turn out, you at least can say that you acted honestly and truthfully to how you felt and what you wanted at that moment. The best part is that I didn't have any expectations and I was detached from the outcome, so it was easier to move pass the situation and keep living my life.

I learned after this experience that guys change their minds and guys can fuck you over, but that is always a possibility when it comes to dating. You can try to weed these assholes out, but in all honesty, you can't be completely sure about someone's intentions. There are always risks when it comes to dating, and you'll get a lot of frogs before you get your prince.

- A WOMAN HAS NEEDS, AND IT'S OKAY TO ACT ON THEM.
- MAKE SURE YOU KNOW WHAT YOU WANT IN A RELATIONSHIP SO YOU'RE NOT SURPRISED BY THE OUTCOME.
- SOME GUYS JUST WANT TO FUCK YOU, AND YOU HAVE TO MAKE SURE THAT YOU'RE OKAY WITH THAT IF YOU CHOOSE TO FUCK THEM TOO.

THE ONE WHO TOOK ME BY SURPRISE

AS A WOMAN who never gives up on love, it's no surprise that I didn't completely shut down after the last experience. If anything, I left with the notion of truly having no expectations because not only did I learn this from my past experiences, but I also didn't have the desire to find someone right away. I've learned that patience is a virtue, and in a society that is programmed for instant gratification, I wanted to challenge myself to not need immediate validation and attention. I was releasing my expectations and wants into the universe because I realized that saying I want something means I lack it, which is a form of resistance. By letting go, I could naturally invite whatever it is that I had been looking for by simply giving up my control.

The end of September was a pivotal time in 2020 because I

was uncovering a lot from my past trauma in my second round of therapy sessions. Just to backtrack a little, I've always been a huge advocate for therapy, but I never actually enrolled in sessions because I knew that it would take commitment to find the right therapist and be consistent in attending sessions. I decided to seek out a therapist when I was grieving over the loss of a friend in July, as I mentioned in the nurse's chapter. After a month of therapy, I stopped going because I wasn't finding value in my sessions.

Two months later, in September, I experienced a lot of anger and frustration all in the span of a few days. I was mislabeling my anger as "anxiety," and I knew I had to give therapy another go. I switched therapists, and I finally realized that my previous therapist wasn't a good fit for me. My current therapist is amazing. She was able to help me notice patterns from my past and unpack a lot of my current issues regarding trust, communication, desire for control, acceptance, etc.

I mention all of this because as I was becoming more vulnerable in my sessions, I felt more comfortable with my past and learned how to reframe the stories I was telling myself. We dove deep into discussing my experience surviving open-heart surgery, and I had never opened up about that part of my life before. It was a very uncomfortable process, but by going into those dark places, I realized that's where the real healing begins. This emotional growth and healing had a direct, positive impact on how I presented myself to the world and how fulfilled I felt as an individual. By addressing my past and everything associated with it—including my fears and insecurities when it came to dating, my anxious, avoidant attachment style, and my hesitancy to speak my mind and state my boundaries—I knew that I would be better equipped to go into a relationship as a more strong-minded person than I ever was in the last twenty-one months of my dating experiences.

And now, this is the right time to introduce you to Mr. Z. We matched on September 15, 2020, and we had a normal introductory exchange of messages. There was something so natural about our flow of conversation that I continued to talk to him on Hinge, which, again, isn't something that I normally do. It was a Tuesday when we had our first conversation on the app. After going back-and-forth for a day or two, I asked if he wanted to grab a drink on Friday. He responded that he couldn't because he had family visiting. He then asked if we could meet up in the following week. But I was leaving for Cancun that Sunday, so we both agreed that we would circle back when I returned.

Similar to my timing with Astronaut, the possibility of us meeting was slim because I always feel like if there's too much time in between matching and meeting up, then it usually won't happen. In my opinion, it's hard to sustain that momentum. Surprisingly, Mr. Z and I remained in contact when I was in Cancun, and I started to realize that I was enjoying our talks even though I was on vacation mode.

When I came back from Cancun, we decided to have our first date, but it wasn't in the traditional sense due to the pandemic. I suggested we could meet for coffee on a Saturday afternoon at 1:30 p.m., which I thought would help us both decide if we got along without the help of alcohol. He lived in Williamsburg, and I lived in East Williamsburg, so I was fond of our close proximity to each other.

Our first date went well, and we ended up talking and roaming around Williamsburg for five hours just getting to know each other. Our coffee interview segment progressed to brunch, and we went to Five Leaves, which is one of my favorite brunch spots in Brooklyn. I was surprised that we were both allowing the natural course of our interaction to unfold on this beautiful Saturday afternoon. I guess it also shows how much both of us missed human interaction, and we weren't going to end the date despite it getting close to sunset. We touched on a wide range of topics including family, relationships, life goals, interests, hobbies, etc. I was pleasantly surprised by how similar we were and how our values aligned seamlessly. We also shared similar family dynamics, and we seemed to be looking for the same thing.

Mr. Z worked for a music label, and I found his passion for his job appealing. He was driven and was essentially living his dream job, which is something I couldn't help but admire. I also liked that he was very much interested in my life, my interests, and my dreams. I never felt like we had a one-sided relationship, and we struck a good balance of talking and listening. I got the sense that he was a really good guy, and I was interested in getting to know more of him.

After our date ended, I thought to myself, *Okay, this guy seems cool.* I wasn't head over heels because it was just the first date. But it was clear to me that we shared common interests and morals, and we had a good foundation for whatever was to come.

I know mentioning that our interests were similar and conversation flowed naturally seems to be redundant in all the chapters, but that's usually the first "test" for me in whether or not the man deserves a second date. I, however, ditched my old habits of creating an imaginary future with the guy in the beginning stages of dating and stopped seeing the situation with rose-colored lenses.

I also didn't want to make the same mistake as I did with the one who screwed me over. I learned from my past experience with the French guy that it's common to find similarities with a guy on a first date, but that does not determine the longevity or success of a relationship.

By this time, Mr. Z and I had already switched to texting, and we continued to talk pretty much daily. We scheduled a second date the following weekend, and we met for drinks at a wine bar in Williamsburg. Unlike our first date, where I was trying to screen him as if he was interviewing for a job, I was much more relaxed, and I started to feel something for Mr. Z. Besides the fact that we just had an undeniable connection, what stood out to me was his curiosity and interest in my life.

I find that too often on dates, we tell each other things because we feel like we have to. The process of getting to know one another seems a bit scripted with cliché topics and questions. Of course, there are some basics that you have to get out of the way, but with Mr. Z, I felt like we were writing our own script instead of following the norm.

He also complimented me throughout the night in ways that I didn't expect. I remembered I was talking about something, and he interrupted me, saying, "Sorry, I just want to say you look beautiful in this light." I remember smiling, taking in what he said, and receiving it with acceptance and thanked him. I don't know if it's because I wasn't used to hearing compliments, but I felt like he wasn't trying to impress me but rather just be present with me. I also realized that my love language changed from quality time in my past relationship to words of affirmation, so he was filling my cup without knowing. After a round of drinks, we decided to grab dinner and be adventurous by going to the city with the hopes of landing a reservation at La Pecora Bianca. I was wearing a white romper, and it was getting chillier throughout the night. We had to wait an hour before getting seated, so we went to another bar to kill some time. When we returned, our table was finally ready, but it was outdoor dining due to the pandemic.

The restaurant was selling fleece blankets and without me requesting one, Mr. Z took it upon himself to ask for one for me because he could tell I was freezing in silence. We had a great dinner as expected, because La Pecora Bianca has the best pasta. It was worth the trip to the city despite it being chilly dining outdoors. We were blessed to also have a live band stop by in the middle of the street to play some music for all of us. The night was going really well, and by the time we finished eating, I think it still hadn't been 11 p.m. By New York standards, this is pretty early. I could've easily called it a night, but I did want to spend more time with him, so we decided to have a drink at his place. I also thought since we both live in Brooklyn, it was easier to go home from his place than the city anyways.

When we got to his apartment, the first thing I noticed was the amazing views of the Manhattan skyline as he lives right by the water. I don't know how I made my way to sitting on top of the kitchen counter, but that's where we shared our first kiss. I actually had been waiting for him to kiss me all night, so it was a special moment for us. I always have to end my night with a cup of tea so I drank that instead of another alcoholic drink. After hanging out for about an hour or so, I decided to call an Uber to head home, as I was getting tired.

Although Mr. Z and I had only gone on two dates, I felt a connection with him that I hadn't felt with another individual in a really long time. I wasn't cautiously putting all my eggs in one basket, but I didn't have any desire to talk with anybody else on Hinge. With the pandemic still going, I also didn't have the capability, time, or energy to try and juggle more men into the mix.

Our third date was probably my favorite date because the theme for it was "adventure"—and as you already know, that's basically my middle name. We met on a Saturday afternoon in Dumbo, and we explored the neighborhood before accidentally making our way to Brooklyn Heights. I had never been to Brooklyn Heights previously and neither had he. It was so lovely to be able to roam around and be mesmerized by the cute buildings, random alleyways, and streets. We also grabbed a drink at a bar and continued getting to know one another.

The best part about our relationship was the effortlessness. Our conversations continued to be so natural, and I felt like I was getting to know more about Mr. Z. Everything that he revealed to me made me more intrigued. I'm usually a planner, but whenever I was with Mr. Z, I let go of that control and just allowed the day to take us where we were meant to go.

After I finished my pinot noir, we continued to stroll through Brooklyn Heights before making our way to Brooklyn Bridge Pier. He asked if I had ever taken the ferry, and I said no. He was raving about it and was excited for me to experience it with him. And the next thing I knew, we were heading for the ferry line and decided to take the next one to South Street Seaport. I loved his spontaneity, and I still have photos from our ferry ride, which happened during sunset, so it brings me right back to the magical moment that we shared. Our ferry ride lasted for about two minutes, and I was shocked by how quickly we arrived in Manhattan.

We didn't have any plans because we were truly just being adventurous. As we strolled around the financial district, we both became a bit hungry and decided our next plan of action was to find some food. After suggesting some neighborhoods, he stopped me as I mentioned Koreatown. We both looked at each other and knew that some Korean food was what we needed.

We took the R train from Cortlandt station and decided to ride 8 stops to 34th street. When we were waiting for our train on the platform, we slow danced without music, and for me, it's the small things like that that pulls my heartstrings. He joked that we were tackling all the different modes of transportation that day as we checked off walking, ferry, and train. And he predicted that traveling by car would be in our future.

Once we went to Koreatown, we walked around the main

strip before settling at Jongro BBQ, and we had an amazing, delicious, and filling dinner. I remember thinking, *Wow, I'm starting to really like this guy, and I'm excited to see where this goes.* What I look for in a guy aside from being loyal, ambitious, and loving is someone who I can always have fun with, and that's exactly what Mr. Z was giving me. I always felt like I was smiling and having the best time, and aren't those the traits that you look for in a best friend and partner? Again, our connection was very strong, and he just understood me in ways that not many men have before.

When we finished our meal, we decided to go back to his place to unwind. We were both craving desserts, so we decided to stop by a cafe we both loved, Gelateria Gentile. When we were waiting in line, I noticed a sign that said "Cash Only," but neither one of us had cash. We were bummed that we couldn't share this gelato moment together, but we didn't give up on our dessert cravings. Instead, we headed over to Van Leeuwen for some ice cream. When we arrived, the line was pretty long, so we thought it would be best to go to the local grocery store and grab some ice cream and eat it at his place.

I remember looking at the frozen aisle, and we were deciding on which ice cream to grab. The peppermint bark ice cream from Talenti stood out to us, and then we wanted something else to go with it. Van Leeuwen pints were right next to it, and I recall telling him when we were going to Van Leeuwen Ice Cream that my go-to flavor is honeycomb. We decided to do honeycomb since that was my original choice to begin with.

We headed back to his apartment, and he did the honors of

scooping ice cream from both pints for me. I never tasted the peppermint bark ice cream before, so as I was digging into my first taste, I asked Mr. Z to pass me the pint because I was curious to know what was in it. A few minutes later, something didn't sit well with me. I started to feel an uncomfortable itch in my mouth and knew what was happening. Your girl was having an allergic reaction!

I asked to see the honeycomb pint and realized that we grabbed the vegan version, which is made of cashew milk. Cashews are one of my nut triggers! I had a mini panic attack but tried to remain as cool, calm, and collected as possible. So for full disclosure, I have a mild nut allergy. And if you're curious, I'm allergic to cashews, pecans, pistachios, and walnuts. Peanuts and almonds are okay, which I know is weird and uncommon. I've experienced a reaction only a handful of times. I know for me personally, it usually wears off after thirty minutes, and my mouth and throat become itchy. And as you can imagine, it's not a pleasant experience, and I don't wish this upon anyone.

The ironic part of all of this was that right before we dug into our ice cream, I playfully quizzed him on what nuts I was allergic to, and he successfully named my four culprits. I tried to disguise my taste buds by drinking water and downing spoonfuls of the peppermint bark ice cream. I could tell that Mr. Z was also freaking out, but I reassured him that I was fine and it would pass.

As we both sat on the couch passing time, he noticed that I was getting uncomfortable. I then started to Google what I could do because it wasn't serious enough for me to go to the emergency room, but it was something I didn't want to ignore. I asked if he could get me Benadryl so he went downstairs to his local deli to retrieve it for me. Luckily, by the time he returned, my discomfort was subsiding, and I felt better.

It was actually a hilarious moment that we shared. I'm sure he will remember it forever, but the upside of that night was that he would never forget what my allergies were again. And in his defense, it wasn't his fault at all even though he took responsibility for it. We both had no idea that Van Leeuwen launched a vegan version of the honeycomb flavor, and to be honest, I should've looked at the ingredients beforehand, knowing that I had allergies.

Either way, I was grateful that I was fine. After that little hiccup in the night, we relaxed and watched *The British Baking Show* on Netflix. There was definitely some sexual tension between us. But I knew that as much as I liked him, I still wanted to make sure that he saw me as a potential partner and not just someone to have sex with, especially after what happened with the French guy. Needless to say, we didn't have sex, and I ended up going home knowing that I had one of the best and memorable dates in my life (minus the allergic reaction moment).

I mentioned during our third date that it would be nice to see him on a weekday if he could fit it in with his work schedule. He was always a good listener and took note of what I said. For example, that following week, we decided to have a Wednesday date because his workload was much lighter than normal, and he wanted to take advantage of that. Though it wasn't as action packed as our previous dates had been, it was just nice to see him during the week. We had a nice dinner at L'Amico. Even though we probably only spent three hours with each other (given that our dates normally lasted at least six hours), I still enjoyed our quality time.

We were now gearing up toward a month of seeing each other, and I knew on my end that I liked him and saw a lot of potential for our relationship. I was doing a spontaneous one-night trip to the Catskills in mid-October, but since we were seeing each other consistently on weekends, I wanted to see Mr. Z the night I was returning.

We decided to grab drinks at Teddy's in Brooklyn, and he showed up with an immense amount of energy and positivity. I was tired from traveling, but his energy was contagious. I wanted to be on the same wavelength as him. To my surprise, after we finished our first round of drinks, he suggested we take tequila shots and told the waitress to bring them out. My initial response was *hell no* because I know what tequila does to my body. But my second thought was, *Why not, let's do it!* I knew I needed the extra energy, and I wanted to just have fun and let loose. Our one shot of tequila turned into two shots, and I was in an *amazing mood*!

We decided to go back to his place and stopped at our usual grocery store to pick up some chocolate. I loved that Mr. Z also had a sweet tooth. He not only supported my dessert cravings, but he also always joined me in indulging. I was definitely tipsy at this point, but I don't think I was drunk. I really wanted to be comfortable because I was wearing boots and jeans that day. If you're like me, the first thing you do when you get home is basically strip naked and change to comfy clothes. Mr. Z went into his closet and gave me cozy, oversized robe from MUJI to change into. The thought of spending the night did cross my mind because I was so comfortable with not only the environment but also with Mr. Z that I didn't completely ignore it. I don't remember what we were watching on television, but one thing led to another and we were heading to his bedroom. I think this is the part where the tequila shots kicked in because I don't remember the night vividly, but what I can confirm is that we had great sex.

This might sound crazy but for the first time, when Mr. Z and I were having sex, I didn't feel like we were having sex. I mean I did, but it was much more than that. I always say that sex is an exchange of energy, but I had never really experienced that notion until that night. I felt so connected and comfortable with Mr. Z that I thought, *Wow, this is something very special that we are sharing right now.* (I obviously didn't say this out loud, but that's what I thought.)

We ended up falling asleep shortly after. I don't want to go into too much details of that night, but what I can say is that we had sex multiple times throughout the night until the morning, and that's something that I cherish. The last time I slept over at a guy's place was when I was with Canadian, but that time was almost a necessary thing for me to realize where I stood with him. Before Canadian, it was years ago when I was in my relationship. So it was such a foreign and new concept for me to wake up with someone next to me, but it was also so refreshing.

Mr. Z made me feel beautiful and special throughout the

night, and I don't think any man has ever made me feel that way before. The way he looked at me gave me confidence and reassurance that what we had was real. I woke up feeling better than I ever had that year, and I was so happy that I was able to experience that moment with him because I honestly forgot what it was like. The best way to describe the feeling is to picture the first scene from *Cinderella* when she wakes up to the sound of birds. She is in the happiest mood and ready to conquer her day.

We barely slept throughout the night, but we decided to get up and take a walk because it was such a lovely Sunday morning. He brought me espresso in bed, and I couldn't get over how comfortable I felt with him. I kept thinking to myself, *Is this what it's like to be in an actual relationship? And is this a glimpse of the "normal life" outside of dating?* We took a nice stroll by the water and continued to have deeper and more meaningful conversations. I was enjoying the pace of our relationship, and everything just felt right. We stopped at Freehold to grab some breakfast and then headed back to his apartment for a relaxing Sunday.

One of my biggest fears was overstaying my welcome because as I mentioned in the chapter with Canadian, I didn't feel wanted. With Mr. Z, however, it was the complete opposite. He told me that we could enjoy each other's company and just see how the day goes. We ended up watching *Bridesmaids*, which is one of my favorite movies of all time, and it was a relaxing way for us to just hang out without any worries or pressure.

My tiredness was slowly kicking in. I knew that I wanted to be home at a reasonable time because it was a Sunday, and Sunday scaries are a real thing. I also wanted to give him time and space to prepare for the week ahead. I ended up leaving around 5 p.m., but I left feeling better than I did going into the night before. Any interaction with a fellow human being—whether it's with your friends, family, or someone you're seeing—should be a positive one. You should leave that conversation or experience feeling better, and if you leave feeling drained or take away any negativity, then that's a warning sign. I knew that my positive mood change was a good sign of how I felt about him and where things were going.

Mr. Z and I continued to talk throughout the week, and Rochelle was visiting me the weekend after. She was leaving Sunday morning, and we had planned to hang out that day. I remember talking very highly of Mr. Z to Rochelle. Now if there's anybody who knows my dating history and basically can write this book herself, it would be Rochelle. She's heard about every single date I've been on, so it was a huge thing for me to tell her that I actually see a future with Mr. Z.

Mr. Z and I were texting throughout the day on Saturday, and then around 5 p.m., he stopped writing back, which left me feeling a bit confused. I wanted to confirm where and when we were meeting on Sunday. I sent him a text around 10 p.m., but I didn't receive an answer. When Sunday came, he sent me a text message in the morning apologizing for his lack of response, and how he went to bed early because he wasn't feeling well. He wanted to postpone our date as he was going to City MD to get a COVID-19 test to make sure everything was fine.

I of course wanted him to take care of his health, so I told him to just update me on his results. Thankfully, his test came back negative, and I was just hoping that he would feel better because I knew he was getting burnt out at work. As we were entering a new week, Mr. Z alerted me that he had a lot on his plate with work considering several of his projects had tight deadlines, which again, I totally understood. Our communication was minimal, but we still kept in touch.

On that Tuesday, I remember texting him and extending an invitation for a home-cooked dinner at my place if he was free on Wednesday or Thursday. He responded that he couldn't swing by due to work. Again, I couldn't and didn't blame him because I knew that he was getting home really late. On Wednesday, he suggested that if I was free on Friday that we could have dinner at his place, and I thought that was a good plan. (I know there's a lot of back-and-forth so try to just follow along.)

When Thursday came around, our communication was minimal to none, and it was the same on Friday. I then received a text from him on Friday, right before noon, and he told me that he needed to postpone the dinner because he had been over his head with work, and he ended up sleeping at his job because that's how late he worked. I also know this wasn't a lie because, as I mentioned earlier, he worked for a music label and there were popular events happening that week.

I always want people to take care of their mental health and bodies so I wrote back completely understanding his situation. I told him to prioritize rest and sleep and to keep me updated if he wanted to hang out during the weekend.

I would be lying if I said I didn't have hopes and expectations that I would see him on Saturday, because I definitely did. Even though we didn't confirm anything on Friday, I thought, *Surely if he takes Friday night to himself and even if he sleeps late, I could at least see him Saturday evening and if not, Sunday.* It had also been two weeks since we'd last spent time together, so it was a given that I wanted to see him.

The last time we spent together, I was at such a high that I felt uneasy when Saturday arrived. I made a mental note to myself that if I didn't hear back from him around 3 p.m. at the latest, there was no chance that I was going to see him that day. And I guess some of you can see where this is going, but 3 p.m. came around and still no text, no nothing.

Where does this leave me? Of course, now being the over-thinker that I am, I'm going through all of these scenarios in my head. A part of me was worried because he usually is a good communicator, so I was wondering if everything was okay. Another part of me was giving him the benefit of the doubt that maybe he truly needed to unplug and unwind and just do absolutely nothing but rest. But the bigger part of me was feeling insecure about the relationship, and I started to fall into the insecure version of myself. I could tell I was tapping into a low frequency. I felt that we had built a great foundation, so I was confused about his silence.

As these thoughts started to present themselves, I started to realize that this scenario was a trigger. A trigger for what you might ask? In my last serious relationship, my boyfriend at the time wanted to take a break to figure things out on his end before agreeing to move in with me. As the people-pleaser that I was at the time, I was okay with him taking a break because I rationalized that he would resent me in the future if I didn't give him time and space to find clarity. That break lasted for about four to five months, which in hindsight, was just ridiculous.

But what I took from that experience was that the uncertainty and being in limbo really doesn't sit well with me. I mean does it for anybody? I think another big part of my relationship with Canadian was that uncertainty factor, and it just ate me up. I'm an all-or-nothing type of gal. But I also know that when it comes to dating, there's a gray area where both individuals are still trying to figure each other out. I didn't need or want Mr. Z to ask me to be his girlfriend. What I needed was some reassurance of how he felt. And in all forms of relationships, communication is key. At this point, there was absolutely no communication, so the only thing I could do was assume.

That afternoon, I was a complete mess, and I felt an extreme influx of emotions. After talking to one of my girlfriends, she told me that this was a rough time not only for him considering what a crazy two weeks he'd had at work, but there was an unsettling feeling in the world with the pandemic and the upcoming election. She gave me a fresh perspective and advised me to not take his actions personally. She warned me that his behavior isn't a reflection of me or the relationship, but it was more based on whatever he was going through.

I realized she was right and felt better after the pep talk, and she told me that if I really wanted to reach out to do so later in the evening, but to keep the focus on him. That's exactly what I did. I texted him the following message around 8 p.m. that Saturday: "Hey just checking in to see how you're doing. I hope you got much-needed rest and sleep today." Was I expecting to hear back? Yes, at least a part of me did because I felt like I was sincere in my approach, and I genuinely wanted to know how he was doing. But did I get a response? Nope.

Sunday comes along and do I hear back? Nope.

Let's take a moment to unpack this. I'm aware that this was an eye-opening situation for me to understand why it bothered me so much. I was able to pinpoint that the anticipation and uncertainty was a trigger for my insecurities and childhood. I was able to see that I was seeking attention and validation from him because I didn't receive this from my past relationships. I was also projecting worst-case scenarios because I was insecure about how he felt about me, given that we also had sex the last time we were together. I started to realize that I was trying so hard to control the outcome that I allowed that to dictate my mood for that weekend. I was setting myself up for failure and misery by holding him to the standards and expectations that I had in my mind.

As Sunday was winding down, I then accepted the reality that he may never text me back. I have a hard time processing how I truly felt this amazing connection with him and things were going so well in the beginning, but I ended up questioning the progression of the relationship and dealing with the fact that this guy I really liked might be ghosting me.

Now, I can't sit here and say that I never ghosted someone before because I am guilty of ghosting people. However, in my defense, the times that I ghosted someone were very much in the earlier stages after the first date, and I didn't want to go out with them again. Sure, it's easier to just tell them that, but I reasoned that it's so early on, there's no attachment so it would be fine. But again, from experience and now in the dating game for more than a year and a half, I can say that ghosting is not cool, and it's not something I intend to do in the future.

I want to be honest and say that I did hold a bit of bitterness not at Mr. Z himself but about the situation. I talked so highly of him to my close friends, and I truly believe in my heart and soul that we had something special. With all that being said, it's really difficult for me to swallow the fact that he didn't have the decency to be honest with me and share what was on his mind. I feel that out of respect for me as a woman and what we shared, he could've at least ended things with me instead of being silent. I would've preferred that he communicate the closing of this relationship than to not respond at all.

It's also hard for me to even write this because I still stand by his character, and I think Mr. Z is a wonderful man. It's difficult for me to unpack the reality of this situation because just a few days before, he was offering to cook me dinner at his place and asked me what I wanted to have. Our conversations were honest, and I felt like he was always genuine with me. Why he chose to not respond to me is something I probably won't ever understand, but like any other dating experience, you learn something from it and you move on. But this one . . . damn, this one hurt.

I thought that was the end of the relationship because everything I have written before was what I thought would be the ending for this chapter, but it turns out there's more.

Mr. Z surprised me when I received a text message from him five days later apologizing and explaining that he had to drive down to see his parents, as there was a COVID-19 scare. He said that he had needed time to focus on that and now he was ready to circle back to his personal life.

I read his message a few times before drafting up a response that was difficult to write, but also one that I'm proud of. I addressed his family situation and acknowledged what he was going through, but I also communicated how his reaction and lack of response didn't sit well with me. I told him that in any relationship, I like and need to be heard and seen. I admitted that I felt hurt when he left me in the dark, especially after I checked in not only once, but three times.

The main reason why I was able to be vocal about my boundaries was due to the lessons I've learned from therapy. My therapist didn't have a good feeling about Mr. Z, but I kept defending our relationship and our connection. I actually had a session with her that Monday. She told me that I have a tendency to repaint people in a positive light, instead of seeing them for who they are. She even quoted Maya Angelou who said, "*When someone shows you who they are, believe them the first time.*" I started to think more about what she said, and that's why I stopped making excuses for Mr. Z, and I began to see the situation for what it was.

Mr. Z responded by taking full responsibility for the situation and sincerely apologized. He recognized that he was in the wrong by not writing back to me and understood why I wanted a response, so I wouldn't get lost in my own thoughts. When we hashed out that situation, we began talking as we normally had previously. At this point, however, I made a mental note because I knew I expressed my needs in a relationship and what my boundaries were, and I wanted to make sure that he was aware of them moving forward.

The following weekend, Biden was the projected 47th president of the USA, and we were all waiting anxiously for the results throughout the week. Mr. Z and I had planned to see each other that night, but with the news being announced in the afternoon, we decided to get together earlier to celebrate.

The energy in Brooklyn was unreal, and everybody was on a high. He called me that Saturday afternoon to ask if I would be okay with grabbing drinks with his friends. Apparently, they had invited both of us. I was down for the celebration, so we met in Williamsburg and barhopped for a few before going back to his place to unwind from the overwhelming day. The day was fun, and we kept it light. We didn't talk about our relationship or dive into an in-depth conversation. The whole date was spent celebrating Biden, and I couldn't complain.

We spoke here and there the following week, and we were planning to meet up again the weekend after. I remember that he canceled on me due to work and was going to reschedule for another day. I don't remember what exactly happened after, but his communication was poor, and I didn't have the energy to follow up as I did the first time. I could just tell that he wasn't emotionally available, and it wasn't fair for me to explore more of this relationship when I knew that dating wasn't a priority in his life at this time.

From his previous response about circling back to his personal life, I realized that his work comes first, and that's okay. I just felt like a second option, and almost like Plan B, so after our last interaction, I made peace with the fact that our relationship would end. He said he would update me on his work, and we would find time to meet, but he never followed up, and we never talked afterward.

Mr. Z is known as the one who took me by surprise because I wasn't expecting to develop feelings for him, and I wasn't expecting for it to end so suddenly without a warning.

However, the only thing I can do in this situation is to look at the positives and take this as a learning opportunity. We are all humans living our own experiences, and we all have different approaches to life and in our relationships. Mr. Z is the last man I'm including in this book, and my relationship with him is the one who I think revealed a lot about my personal growth.

I already mentioned that I was diving deep into my therapy sessions when I was also seeing Mr. Z, so I gained a lot of insight and confidence by how I approached the relationship. As you can probably tell from all my previous experiences, I didn't know what boundaries were. I didn't know what my boundaries were, and when I did learn what those were, I didn't know how to communicate them. I didn't think my boundaries were valid, and I didn't know how to honor them. I was afraid that I was coming off too strict or mean, and I thought my boundaries might push a man away. Now I realize that having boundaries is necessary. Boundaries are a way to protect yourself, and boundaries serve as a way to set the tone for a relationship. I can see the immense progress that I've made from my first date with Brooklyn to my last date with Mr. Z. I was able to vocalize my feelings, and I didn't abandon my boundaries for the sake of being with someone. That observation in itself is something I am proud of. I am walking away a more refined version of myself, and it's all due to what my experiences have taught me.

KEY LESSONS

- DON'T FALL IN LOVE WITH POTENTIAL.
- SOMETIMES WHAT YOU NEED CAN'T BE MET BY WHAT SOMEONE CAN GIVE YOU (AND VICE VERSA), BUT THAT DOESN'T MEAN THEY DON'T CARE.
- SOMEONE GHOSTING IS A SIGN OF:
  - NOT BEING COMFORTABLE WITH CONFRONTATIONS
  - FEAR OF HURTING OTHERS
  - THEIR FAMILIARITY WITH HOW TO END RELATIONSHIPS
- ANOTHER PERSON'S BEHAVIOR AND ACTIONS ARE NOT A REFLECTION OF YOU, BUT RATHER THEIR OWN INSECURITIES, UNHEALDED TRAUMA, CHILDHOOD WOUNDS, OR PAST EXPERIENCES.

- SOME PEOPLE AREN'T READY FOR YOU, AND THAT'S OKAY BECAUSE YOU'RE MAKING SPACE FOR THOSE WHO ARE.

CONCLUSION

WITHIN THE LAST TWENTY-TWO MONTHS of dating, have I found my person? Nope. Have I given up? Not at all. Do I still have hope in this process? Yes.

As you can see, I've met several stand-up guys in the process. All the men I've dated have taught me something, and that's all I can ask for. I also think the best part is that I've grown throughout this journey, and self-development is something that I wouldn't give up for all that I had to go through. My dating journey has been exhausting, overwhelming, and sometimes frustrating, but through it all, it's also been fun, exciting, rewarding, and refreshing.

Now that I'm older and wiser, I'm more comfortable setting boundaries, and I know this new skill set will prove very beneficial for me going into new relationships. I also realized that you can change your mind about what you're looking for in relationships. I've gone through phases thinking I wanted something serious, just to realize later that I actually didn't. I've also just wanted to have fun, but then I realized I wanted something more. There have been times when I wanted something more casual, and there were other times when I wanted something more meaningful.

The most important takeaways I learned from dating is to figure out what you want in a relationship, what your deal-breakers are, what your non-negotiables are, and to always make sure you stand by them no matter what. As I was writing and editing this book, I could see my patterns in how I was selecting these men, why I was attracted to them, why I put up with some of their actions, and why things ended the way they did. I've learned that choosing a person is one of the most important decisions I'll make in my life, so there is no way I am going to settle or rush this process.

I've decided to also not put too much pressure on myself in finding love, because I know as I am continuously working on myself, I will attract someone who is on the same wavelength as me. I am now putting more emphasis on qualities that are the foundation of a good partnership instead of focusing on surface level details. There are some criteria like job titles and skills that are nice to have, but they aren't necessary to be in a healthy and happy relationship.

Before deciding to write this book, I always said I wanted to make the most of this life I've been given. We hear it time and time again that we only have one life to live, and it is often said that we need to appreciate every moment because we can't get them back. But if I take a moment to truly wrap my head around that reality, I think, *Holy fuck, it's so fucking true.* I wake up every day with a fire in me, and I am consistently motivated by accomplishing what's on my bucket list as well as my fear list. I am driven to release all the what-ifs, to get out of my comfort zone, to experience everything there is to experience, and to just live my fucking best life. It's funny that I also adopted this metaphor that we are all writing a book in our lives before actually deciding to finally write this book. I used to say I want to have stories for days. Also, I don't just want my book to have exciting chapters, but rather, I want to expand my chapters into volumes and a full series. Take a moment now, and think about your life. What's your book about? What stories stand out to you? How many chapters have you written? Can you write more?

Recounting these twelve standout moments from my dating history, it's important to also know that I went on a million other dates in between. I didn't mention some random ones as they didn't make the cut. But while I'm wrapping this book up, I thought I would include some of the unique experiences I've had and the men I've matched with and dated through giving online dating a chance:

- **THE ONE WHO SENT AN UNSOLICITED DICK PIC TO ME ON THE FIRST TEXT (AND HIS DICK WASN'T EVEN BIG)**

- THE ONE WHO ASKED IF I WANTED TO JOIN HIM AND HIS SIGNIFICANT OTHER IN SOME FUN
- THE ONE WHO HAD A FULL-ON COLORED BACK TATTOO THAT STARTED FROM HIS SHOULDER BLADES AND WENT ALL THE WAY DOWN TO HIS BUTTOCKS
- THE ONE WHO DIRECTED A VERY WELL-KNOWN NETFLIX SERIES ON DRUGS AND THE CARTEL
- THE ONE WHO REALLY NEEDED SOMEONE TO LISTEN TO HIM, AND THEREFORE, I BECAME HIS THERAPIST
- THE ONE WHO JUST WANTED TO SMOKE WEED WITH ME AND WHO ALSO HAPPENS TO BE THE BROTHER OF A VERY WELL-KNOWN ACTOR
- THE ONE WHO HAD A BEAUTIFUL APARTMENT IN UNION SQUARE, WHERE I WAS MORE INTERESTED IN LIVING IN HIS PLACE THAN GETTING TO KNOW HIM
- THE ONE WHO DIDN'T JOIN ME FOR DRUNK FOOD BUT WATCHED ME DEVOUR A WHOLE SLICE OF PRINCE STREET PIZZA AND SUCCESSFULLY STAIN MY CLOTHES FROM EATING SO MESSILY
- THE ONE WHO SHAMED ME FOR NOT OFFERING TO PAY FOR THE FIRST TWO DATES
- THE ONE WHO ASKED TO SPLIT THE CHECK ON OUR FIRST DATE EVEN THOUGH HE ASKED ME OUT IN THE FIRST PLACE (ALSO, HE ATE MOST OF THE FOOD AND HAD MORE DRINKS THAN I DID.)

It's been a hell of a ride, but hey I wouldn't have wanted to spend my late twenties any other way. While I was dating all of these men, I was also dating myself in the process. We as humans are evolving and growing every day, so it's okay to see relationships change and take their course, too. I've learned to let go of control and expectations. When I was able to detach myself from the outcome, I was better able to let things be. At the end of the day, I can't force love. Love will happen, and love will come. I still believe in love, and I think I always will. The best thing I can say throughout my dating experience is that I'm putting myself out there, I'm taking risks, I'm trying, and I'm following my heart.

When I entered the online dating world, I wanted to find love and be in a relationship, but I didn't know what that relationship with look like or feel like. Today, I know exactly what I want, and that's to be in a healthy, conscious, and growth-oriented relationship. I never imagined I could be so sure of what I'm looking for and I can only owe it to the men I've dated, the breakthroughs I had in my therapy sessions, and the inner work I've done within the last few years.

Though I haven't found my perfect match, let's see how many other dates and men I'll have to meet before I find the one. Until then, who knows, maybe I'll meet more who will make it in another book, or maybe the next person will be the one. Either way, I hope you all felt entertained while I put my business on paper. I hope that you took something valuable from this book, whether you agree with the key lessons or if you learn what not to do from my personal experiences.

This book is a chapter of my real life and a real glimpse of the stage I was at in the mid-late twenties living in New York City. Had I not put myself out there and had not said yes to all these men, I wouldn't have had the crazy experiences I did. And to be honest, looking back, they actually make me smile because I can now pinpoint who Mariann was when she was dating as a single woman in NYC.

Whether you are in a relationship or not, whether you have found your person or not, remember that you are special, you are worthy, and you are meant for something greater than what's on a dating profile, and your time will come.

Whether you're frustrated with dating or whether you're thinking about giving love another chance, remember it takes courage to put yourself out there. It takes courage to open up, to feel vulnerable, and to risk getting hurt. Overcoming heart-break, insecurities, and fears isn't easy—trust me, I know. You're doing the best you can, and I want you to know that I feel you and I see you.

When all else fails, you can resort to the saying, "*It's you, it's not me,*" and just keep trucking along, because I'm here with you. Your girl's got you.

MARIANN YIP is a native New Yorker and was born and raised in the Lower East Side in the beautiful city that never sleeps. She is a lifestyle and travel blogger who shares tips and travel adventures at www.mariannyc.com. She hosts the podcast *The City Confessions*, in which she leads ongoing discussions with other New York residents to share their truths and stories. Mariann's mission is to create a safe platform for storytelling and to normalize pain, struggle, and vulnerability.

In her spare time, Mariann loves traveling to new destinations and getting to know different cultures, checking off her Yelp restaurant bucket list, researching new and cool activities to do in NYC, and exploring new cafés to get her oat milk latte fix. *Un-Hinged* is her first book.